Footprint

Reykjavík

Laura Dixon

Contents

Listings

About the author

Laura Dixon is a travel journalist based in southwest England; specializing in Iceland and France. She read English at Somerville College, Oxford; journalism at the London College of Printing; and Icelandic at college in Reykjavík. She has contributed to several guidebooks about the UK for Itchy guides, Footprint Handbooks and City Life Publishing, in addition to writing for a range of magazines and newspapers. Her favourite place in the world is the Grái Kötturinn café in Reykjavík.

The natives have cheekbones so sharp they can draw blood, the local word for cloud is *ský*, rotten shark meat is considered a delicacy and *Ketill*, meaning 'kettle', is a popular boys' name. It's life through the looking glass – welcome to the topsy-turvy world of Reykjavík.

To the west the cold expanse of the Atlantic Ocean stretches on towards Greenland; to the east mossy lava plains meet bare orange mountains, hot springs and the largest desert in Europe. Reykjavík is a city that feels like it's sprung up from nowhere, where modern architecture reflects the aurora borealis in the winter sky and you can bathe outdoors in the geothermal pools breathing clear, pure air straight from the glaciers. The country's location on the Mid-Atlantic Ridge has generated an independent, vibrant and creative environment where nature is forever active with volcanoes, earthquakes and hot springs.

Northern exposure

The city cherishes its position as the northernmost capital city in the world, out of reach of convention. Being so far off the European map has practically been a licence to be unusual, quirky and ground-breaking in many areas from music to pop art and lifestyles. But behind the futuristic hairstyles and ethereal music lies a city well-grounded in history and folklore. If you counted up all the elves and *huldufólk*, or hidden people, that are said to exist in the Reykjavík suburb of Hafnarfjörður, the small town would take on the dimensions of any other European city.

Nature or culture

The strangeness of everyday life is mirrored in Reykjavík's surreal natural beauty. It's so far north that the sun, like the locals, barely sleeps in summer, dipping briefly into the sea in the early hours of the morning. In the winter it sleeps off a long hangover of its own. Peering out across the Faxaflói Bay, past the old whalers, you can usually catch a glimpse of Snæfellsjökull, the magical glacier which has inspired writers for centuries with a sense of its mystery. Closer still, Mount Esja looms purple, mauve and pink against a bloodshot sky at sunset, its snow-dusted peak changing colour with every passing season.

A place apart

Reykjavík is a city for dreamers, fantasists and individuals. Somewhere you can lose yourself in the Viking Age sagas of independent thinkers who rewrote the laws their way; visit the national park, Þingvellir, which is growing at a rate of around 2 cm a year; or admire Iceland's creative flair in one of the city's sculpture galleries. Icelanders have the highest standard of living and longest life expectancy of all of Europe's citizens. The beer might be expensive but the air is clean, creativity is a way of life and you'll go home with a different perspective. Out here, it's the only one they have.

At a glance

Reykjavík is a small town by anyone's standards. Capital of a country the size of England and Wales together, the city comprises approximately 40% of the country's meagre population of 280,000, making it the island's only real city and the cultural centre of everything in Iceland. The attractions of coming here are twofold: for the countryside within easy reach of the city, alive with geological faults; and for the lifestyle in the city, young, vibrant and earth-shaking in its own way.

101 Reykjavík

The bohemian old town of Reykjavík is situated between two water features – the harbour and the pond. In between the two you'll find the centrepoint of the city, Austurvöllur Square, with the historic Alþing parliament building and city cathedral, and some welcoming cafés on its borders. Follow the main street, Austurstræti, up the hill and it becomes Laugavegur, the main shopping street. Above it on the hill is Hallgrímskirkja, a towering church designed to look like an erupting volcano – man, god and nature combined in almost frightening grandeur. Running quietly off Laugavegur is Hverfisgata, a row of corrugated-iron houses in bright, primary colours with a lived-in appeal and wonderful views down to the water and beyond to Mount Esja. Down by the harbour you'll find the flea market at weekends with a fish hall at the back and, occasionally, fairground rides along the quayside, complete with children clutching those perennial favourites – candyfloss, *pylsur* and dried cod.

Laugardalur Valley and Öskjuhlíð Hill

On the outskirts of the city you'll find two of Reykjavík's most idiosyncratic sights. Laugardalur Valley is the centre of Iceland's sporting activity and a bit of a hotspot. The name refers to the hot springs, now used to feed the city's biggest swimming pool, with steam room, Olympic-sized outdoor pool and luxury spa complex. Öskjuhlíð Hill has got the look of a secret military hideout built on the foundations of an old Second World War base, but the spherical Pearl building was not designed to be hidden, perched as it is like a broody hen on top of six round tanks that store the city's hot water. It's the nearest thing the city has to the Eiffel Tower, with viewpoints out over the city and beyond, and a nice café inside, as well as a historical museum. At the very top there's a revolving gourmet restaurant and a fabulous bar, but both are prohibitively expensive even by Icelandic standards. Down at the foot of the hill you'll find a yellow-sand beach, hot pots and a warmed-up section of the Atlantic that you can swim or paddle in.

Hafnarfjörður and the Blue Lagoon
On the Reykjanes Peninsula to the west of Reykjavík are two sights that make use of the natural surroundings. The dark, bumpy, moss-covered lava fields around Hafnarfjörður in particular have given rise to numerous stories about elves, pixies and angels, and a reputation for being home to the biggest otherworldly community in the country. And beyond it towards Keflavík is the world-famous Blue Lagoon, a steaming pool of opaque turquoise water that leaches minerals from the lava bed, filling it with healing properties. Here you can lie back, put a mud pack on your face, relax and try not to let that whiff of sulphur put you off.

The Golden Circle: Þingvellir, Gullfoss and Geysir
The Golden Circle is a day tour of three of Iceland's natural wonders, only about 50 km from the city. Passing through the small town of Mosfellsbær you reach Þingvellir, seated firmly on the Mid-Atlantic Ridge which swoops diagonally through the

country, northeast from the capital. At Þingvellir you can actually see the Eurasian and American continental plates draw apart from each other. From here you can get to Geysir, an area of spouting hot springs which gave its name to all such natural features the world over, and Gullfoss, a huge two-step waterfall that partially freezes in winter.

Akureyri, the Snæfellsnes Peninsula, Landmannalaugar and the Westman Islands

Beyond Reykjavík is a whole new world of lava fields, fjords and glaciers. Akureyri, the second largest city in the north of the country, is at the end of Iceland's longest fjord surrounded by a national park and provides the opportunity to reach the island of Grímsey on the Arctic Circle. The Snæfellsnes Peninsula, closer to Reykjavík, has an inspirational glacier, coastal walks and an impressive array of birdlife. Landmannalaugar in the central highlands is an area of outstanding beauty, with orange rhyolite mountains and a hot spring for outdoor bathing, as well as being the start point for one of Iceland's most spectacular hikes. Finally, the Westman Islands off the south coast have two volcanoes, walking trails and a host of puffin catchers in the summer months. The archipelago includes the island of Surtsey which emerged 40 years ago in a submarine volcanic eruption.

Trip planner

Reykjavík is one of the smallest capital cities in the world and it's easy to find your way around. A long weekend is time enough to sample the city, nightlife and culture as well as marvel at the surrounding otherworldly landscape on a day trip. Three-day stopovers on flights from Europe to the US and vice-versa on Icelandair are the ideal opportunity to see the country. Visit the countryside, bathe in the hot springs and try some of the outstanding cuisine before flying on, relaxed and refreshed.

With a week you can make the most of your stay and travel up to the north of the country for the dramatic scenery of the fjords and lakes. You can negotiate the city very quickly as it's only the size of a small town, but it would take a few days to explore all the areas thoroughly. Pace yourself, relax in a café or two in between galleries and museums, and spend at least a day in the countryside to balance it out.

The high season for travel is June to August when there's a lot of sunlight (the sun rises at around 0300 and sets at 2400), although not always sunshine, and temperatures are an average of 11°C. Prices drop considerably in September, but then so too do the hours of sunlight. In December the sun rises around 1120 and sets at 1530. During the winter you can see the Northern Lights and take glacier trips, but things are a little colder and some attractions are closed. If you're coming specifically to see seabirds or whales, July is the best time of year; for the Northern Lights you need to come from September to March.

A weekend

Make the most of the unpolluted air by having a **relaxing and reviving weekend**. Take a tour to Landmannalaugar, a few hours drive away by bus or Land Rover, where you can bathe in natural hot springs in the middle of nowhere. Take a walk around Þingvellir at your own pace, admiring the natural scenery and history. If you're in

★ **Ten of the best**

1 **National Museum of Iceland** Tangible exhibitions and multimedia displays provide a fascinating insight into 1200 years of Icelandic history and culture, p44.

2 **Hallgrímskirkja** The tall, pale, volcano-shaped church in the centre of Reykjavík with views out to Faxaflói Bay from the steeple on a clear day, p49.

3 **Nauthólsvík Beach** Reykjavík's own beach, heated with geothermal water, p65.

4 **The Blue Lagoon** A 39°C bowl of milky-blue soup in the lava fields of the Reykjanes Peninsula with healing properties and an ethereal, otherworldly feel, p80.

5 **Þingvellir National Park** Where you can see the earth being created in front of your eyes, p84.

6 **Geysir and Gullfoss** Much-visited natural wonders where you can see water leap high into the air, and a wide and beautiful two-step waterfall half-frozen in winter and veiled with rainbows and mist in summer, p87 and p89.

7 **Snæfellsjökull** This glacier was the inspiration for novels by Jules Verne and Halldór Laxness. There's plentiful birdlife and a few alien life forms out here too, p93.

8 **Landmannalaugar** A natural hot spring surrounded by multicoloured rhyolite mountains and fields of shiny obsidian, p96.

9 **The Westman Islands** Home to thousands of puffins that leave in August, but outside the puffin season you can still see the odd whale or active volcano, p99.

10 **Lava by horseback** Get a feeling for the outback by trekking with one of the friendly Icelandic horses across the folklore-inspiring moonscape, p195.

The ★ symbol is used throughout the guide to indicate these recommended sights.

Reykjavík in winter, a Northern Lights tour is highly recommended, just out of the city where the greenish hues light up the sky. Finally, get close to nature on a whale-watching tour in late summer when there's a good chance of seeing minke whales just offshore, and relax in the Blue Lagoon before flying home.

For an **all-action weekend**, spend your first day exploring the outdoors with a friendly native guide – the Icelandic horse. There are a number of tour companies to take you out to nearby lavascapes (see p195), or try a husky-dog tour on a glacier. You could also arrange a whitewater rafting trip in south Iceland to get your adrenaline pumping, then relax your aching muscles in one of the city's thermal baths. The following day, take a trip to Þingvellir and go caving (see p31). A couple of tour companies can take you down into what feels like the centre of the earth where the tectonic plates are moving apart into lava caves. If organized tours aren't your thing, hire a Land Rover and drive to Kleifarvatn on the Reykjanes Peninsula to see the geothermal area and experience driving through the lava landscape.

Reykjavík has a funky, offbeat atmosphere making it the perfect place for an **art-house weekend** break. The film *101 Reykjavík* was filmed in *Kaffibarinn* on Laugavegur, so drop in there for a coffee during the day. Visit the city's art galleries, particularly Kjarvalsstaðir and the Harbour House Museum. Friday and Saturday nights are the liveliest nights of the week – especially after midnight – in the stylish downtown bars. And don't forget to try *brennivín*, the local firewater with a kick like a mule and guaranteed to have you making an ass of yourself. For live Icelandic music, try *Gaukur á Stöng* on Tryggvagata any night of the week. A browse through shops on Skólavörðstígur can ease your hangover and hiring a car to get out into the countryside around Reykjavík will give you some inspiration of your own.

A **weekend without breaking the bank** is possible in Reykjavík. Most museums have free admission one day a week. The Reykjavík Tourist Card is also a cheap way of getting around museums, galleries and swimming pools with discounts and free bus fares. Thermal baths are cheap at ISK 250 and well worth relaxing in for an afternoon, as are coffee shops where you can soak up the atmosphere and check out the latest haircuts. The beach and Pearl are both free to visit. Complete your weekend by taking a trip to one of the natural wonders. Live music is often free or around ISK 500, a cheap and entertaining night out if you don't hit the beer too hard.

A week

If you're in Reykjavík for a week it makes sense to venture out of the city. Plan your time carefully so that you're in the city for the nightlife on Friday and Saturday night and arrange a few days out in the beautiful countryside of Akureyri in the north of the country. It takes 40 minutes to fly there and from the town you can reach the island of Grímsey, sitting astride the Arctic Circle. On your return to Reykjavík, there will be plenty of time to explore the museums and bars of the town.

Take a trip to Vestmannaeyjar, the Westman Isles. There you can see a volcano, whales and puffins – depending on the season – and some of the friendliest of the Icelandic people. Alternatively, take a trip to Snæfellsnes, visit the glacier and see the wonderful birdlife. If you like walking, the Laugavegur walking trail from Landmannalaugar to the forest of Þorsmörk in south Iceland is well known and very popular, taking around three to four days in total. To fit everything in, go back to Keflavík Airport via the Blue Lagoon where you can relax ready for your trip home.

Contemporary Reykjavík

Reykjavík has found a special place in the heart of the world's media for being as weird as green toast. Yet the capital city inexplicably finds itself forgotten by the world because it's tucked away in the frozen north and frequently gets left off European maps. That's no surprise to the rest of Europe who see it as an isolated enigma, but to the well-travelled and generally cosmopolitan locals who see themselves as a stepping stone between America and Europe, it's a bit wide of the mark.

Reykjavík knows it's unique and that life here is very different to that in any town of similar size anywhere else in the world. The city is set in an expanse of lava fields, close to both the largest desert and biggest glacier in Europe. These natural influences, added to the long, dark, mean winters, have both shaped and inspired the inhabitants. People here are, for the most part, highly creative and every second person seems to be a writer, musician or artist. The proportion of the population under 30 in rock bands explains how it's possible to find live music in the city every night of the week. The Reykjavíkurs cherish their independence and difference from the rest of Europe very dearly, ready to show their pride in the country by dressing in the latest fashions, not text-book copycat like in some parts of Europe, but fully expressing their individuality.

The same can be said of the city's modern architecture and art scene. Reykjavík has a comparatively large number of sculpture gardens, mainly dating from the 19th century, containing both abstract and realistic representations of the Saga myth stories on which the nation's culture is founded. Ásmunder Sveinsson's collection, for example, is a garden containing a sprawling voluptuous Viking, while Einar Jónsson's garden has more of a Gothic, hallucinogenic overtone.

The way in which the medieval history of the country has been preserved through the saga manuscripts is unique to Iceland. It's safe to say that no other country has its thousand-year-old memory preserved in calfskin manuscripts. Icelanders have been able to trace their genealogies through the manuscripts. Not only that but new genetics technology has been used to analyse patterns of inherited genes amongst almost the entire community.

This history is being constantly reinterpreted today by artists in all genres re-examining their cultural identity. The ambient rock group Sigur Rós, underground favourites with as diverse a following as Tom Cruise in the States and Thom Yorke in the UK, have set an old Icelandic form of ballad, known as *rímur*, to music. And among his many achievements, Nobel-prize winning novelist Halldór Laxness examined the hardships experienced by the farming community and the difficulties inherent in the modernization of rural Iceland. In *Independent People*, his most famous novel, he reminds Iceland to think about its future as well as its past.

Reykjavík retains aspects of this rural past, having only really grown up into a city since the early 19th century. Commercial fishing is the major industry, with farming and tourism providing additional income. As the seas become overfished and yields begin to drop, fishermen are facing the unpalatable reality that this kind of industry cannot be sustained indefinitely. Farmers likewise are bowed by commercial pressures and quotas. The country seems unlikely to relinquish its fishing territory by joining the EU but at the same time can't risk being left behind and out of European decisions as this industry declines. The debate about sacrificing its proud independence to become a fully fledged EU member has been rumbling on for some time and is becoming a case of when, not if.

Living off the land isn't a long-term prospect but Iceland has found some ways of harnessing what it has to offer. Geothermal energy heats the majority of houses in the city and the raging rivers are harnessed for electricity, making this a very green way of living.

! When the Vikings arrived in Iceland 60% of the country was covered in grass, bushes and trees. Thanks mainly to over-grazing by sheep, a third of the country is now officially desert.

Keeping Iceland Green

Iceland is envied by many for its clean air and unpolluted wild spaces – including Europe's largest glacier and largest desert. With a small population, little heavy industry and an abundance of geothermal and hydroelectric power, the country leads the way in environmentally-friendly energy production. Yet its precious natural environment has a slightly uncertain future.

While about 70% of Iceland's energy comes from clean and renewable resources – the largest percentage of any developed country – the low costs of production have been central in procuring foreign investment and business opportunities in the form aluminium smelters and massive dams. What's more, Iceland's reliance on geo-thermal power makes it exempt from the Kyoto Protocol's ruling on fossil fuel emissions. This means that Icelandic industries can operate without having to pay penalties for carbon dioxide emissions.

While foreign investment in an economy heavily reliant fishing and tourism is welcome, industrial growth has been so rapid that some longer term issues have yet to be addressed and the Icelandic people have begun to ask questions about the potential abuse of their natural assets. In recent years, hunger strikes and protests across the country have raised awareness of the real cost of foreign investment – the long term health of their natural world.

While Iceland aims to be the first country to dispose of fossil fuels and is at the forefront of developing alternative forms of transport such as hydrogen-powered vehicles, it now needs to harmonize the viewpoints of energy production and environmental protection. The time has come for Iceland to turn green.

Recently the Icelandic government has found an additional use for this huge amount of readily available energy by introducing aluminium and steel smelters. The metals are imported but the processing costs foreign companies less because the cost of energy is so low. Oil and petrol are now only really used to power the fishing trawlers, and the many cars and 4WDs around the town.

Not only is the air cleaner than most other places on the planet, children are also allowed to grow up here in one of the safest of environments, playing in the streets and playgrounds in the knowledge that nothing will harm them in this extremely child-friendly society. It is noticeable that people have children here very early, usually in their twenties, and the Reykjavíkurs have an incurably healthy view about parenthood. It's seen as part of life rather than the end of your youth, and dovetails in neatly with everything else.

Mix in the fact that the majority of the population is middle class and Reyjavík appears to have the recipe for a perfect society, but there may be storm clouds on the horizon. The city and the country in general are beginning to have to deal with the kind of social problems that affected other European nations years ago: immigration, unemployment and a growing army of teenagers, bored with small-town claustrophobia and turning to drugs and violence. What's more, the decision to resume commercial whaling has outraged foreign governments and environmental groups and divided public opinion. With tourism playing an increasingly important part in the country's economy, Iceland cannot afford to alienate itself from the international community.

Reykjavík is currently undergoing a vast amount of change as it runs to catch up with the rest of the world. It relishes its position in the world as the capital of cool but is seeking to embrace this new-found inclusion without allowing it to influence its eccentric spirit too much. Although things are changing fast, the city is not ready to relinquish its special status just yet. Reykjavík may feel like it's about to lose its innocence but it is still more than anxious to retain its character, history and culture.

Iceland can be reached by air and sea. Keflavík International Airport is 48 km from Reykjavík city centre and the most popular point of entry. By sea, the port of Seyðisfjörður is 682 km from the city on the eastern coast of Iceland. Negotiating the city is very easy. There are four options: your feet, the reliable yellow Stræto buses which run every 20 minutes during the day, hiring a bike, or fighting your way along the busy streets in a car. There is neither a rail nor a metro system because Reykjavík simply doesn't need it.

There are a huge number of trips you can take from Reykjavík into the weird and wonderful countryside. Þingvellir, the Blue Lagoon, Gullfoss and Geysir are unmissable and can be done either as part of an organized group or by hire car. Reykjavík is very safe at all times of day and night. If you arrive after midnight you'll certainly find somewhere to drink, but eating is a problem as most places close at 2200. Most hotels are open 24 hours but in general guesthouses will be shut by midnight unless you've arranged with them to stay open later prior to arrival.

Getting there

Air

Icelandair, **T** 505 0372, www.icelandair.is, is the major carrier to Keflavík International Airport and has a regular schedule of daily non-stop flights to Iceland from Europe and North America. It's also possible to stop over in Iceland for a maximum of three days when crossing the Atlantic. All prices are for return flights without tax and are subject to availability. Discounts of up to 50% are available online.

Iceland Express, **T** 550 0600, www.icelandexpress.is, is a budget airline flying daily from the UK, Denmark and Germany (high season only), with further European routes starting in 2006. Prices start from £69/€99 and go as high as £210/€300 with the majority of fares around the £105/€150 mark. Special fares as low as £5/€7 are sometimes available.

From UK and Ireland Icelandair, Adam House, 2nd floor, 1 Fitzroy Square, London, W1T 5PE, **T** 0870-7874020, flies from Glasgow and London Heathrow airports. From Heathrow there are two flights daily (three hours, from £236/£102 online). From Glasgow there are four flights a week (two hours 10 minutes, from £256/£99 online). From April 2006, there will be two flights a week from Manchester (£256/£102 online). Discounts are available for students and anyone under 26 from **STA Travel**, www.sta.com. **Iceland Express**, **T** 0870-2405600, flies daily from London Stansted.

From North America Icelandair flies to Iceland from a number of North American cities. The prices below refer to the weekday/weekend price. Peak season runs from 26 May to 17 August. There are six flights a week from Boston (five hours, peak season US$982/1042, off-peak US$763/823), six from Baltimore-Washington Airport (six hours 20 minutes, peak season US$1050/1110, off-peak US$831/891), four from Minneapolis-St Paul Airport (six hours, peak season US$1096/1156, off-peak US$875/935), three from Orlando, Florida (seven hours 10 minutes, peak season US$1096/1156, off-peak US$875/935) and daily flights from New York (five hours 20 minutes, peak season US$983/1042, off-peak US$763/823). From May 2006 there will be three flights a week from San Francisco during summer only (eight hours 20 minutes, peak season US$1096/1156, off-peak US$875/935).

From Europe Icelandair flies directly to Keflavík from Amsterdam, Barcelona, Berlin, Copenhagen, Frankfurt, Milan, Oslo, Paris and Stockholm. There are four flights weekly from Amsterdam (three hours, €385), one flight weekly from Barcelona (summer only, four hours 15 minutes, €551), three flights weekly from Berlin (summer only, three hours 20 minutes, €380), up to three flights daily from Copenhagen (three hours 10 minutes, peak season DKK 2600, off-peak DKK 2225), four flights a week from Frankfurt (three hours 35 minutes, €380), two flights a week from Milan (summer only, four hours 15 minutes, €646), daily flights from Oslo (two hours 40 minutes, peak season NOK 3020, off-peak NOK 2755), daily flights from Paris, (three hours 25 minutes, €376) and daily flights from Stockholm (three hours 10 minutes, peak sesason SEK 3125, off-peak SEK 2855). After 26 October the frequency of these flights drops until the beginning of June.
Iceland Express flies daily from Copenhagen. From 2006, Iceland Express will also be flying from Alicante, Berlin, Stockholm, Friedrichshafen and Gothenburg.

Airport information Keflavík International Airport (KEF), **T** 425 0600, www.airport.is, has only one terminal and shares a runway with a NATO base. In the arrivals hall you'll find a telephone, 24-hour bank and cash point, money exchange, tourist information centre and various car hire firms. There is a café on the second floor and a taxi rank outside arrivals. A taxi to central Reykjavík costs around ISK 8000 (see Directory, p217). The reliable **Flybus**, **T** 562 1011, www.flybus.is, meets incoming flights and

Travel extras

Business hours Standard office hours are Monday to Friday 0800-1600. Banks are generally open Monday to Friday 0915-1600 and post offices from Monday to Friday 0830-1630. Shops open Monday to Friday 0900-1800 and often on Saturday morning. Supermarkets and petrol stations stay open until 2300.

Climate Iceland is on the Gulf Stream so it's warmer than it feels it should be this far north. The average temperature in the summer is 11°C and in the winter it's 0°C, but colder out towards the glaciers and further north, and there can be a fair amount of cloud and rain at all times of year which can strike you from the horizontal as well as from above. The weather changes frequently so waterproofs, warm gear and sunscreen should always be carried. Always check the weather forecast, www.vedur.is/english, or telephone **T** 568 9200 or **T** 060 044 for a forecast in English.

Money The Icelandic currency is the Icelandic Kroner (ISK). At the time of writing € 1 = ISK 78, UK £1 = ISK 114, US $1 = ISK 63. As long as you have a compatible credit/debit card and sufficient funds, using an ATM is the most convenient way of keeping in funds, but check bank charges. Iceland is a relatively expensive country to visit and the minimum daily budget for food and accommodation only will be around ISK 6000, rising to as much as ISK 20,000 for more upmarket tastes.

Telephone The IDD code for Iceland is +354. All numbers have seven digits and there are no area codes. See also p217.

Visas Citizens of EU countries, most European countries and North America are exempt from visa requirements for up to 90 days.

drops you at your hotel, guesthouse or hostel. They also go from the city to Keflavík airport five times a day, picking up at major hotels and guesthouses two hours before outgoing flights. It costs

ISK 1150 one-way. There's a duty-free shop selling alcohol at reasonable prices for people flying in as well as out of the country, and as Iceland isn't part of the EU, duty-free hasn't been abolished here. For late-evening arrivals there isn't much beyond the odd car rental place open, but there is a benefit in arriving late as you'll arrive at Reykjavík at about the time that the place starts getting ready to party. Domestic air terminals: Reykjavík Airport, **T** 570 8090; Akureyri Airport, **T** 460 7000; Heimaey Airport, **T** 481 3255.

Sea
From Europe Smyril Line, J Broncksgøta 37, PO Box 370, FO-110 Tórshavn, Faroe Islands, **T** +298-345900, www.smyril-line.com, runs ferries to the port of Seyðisfjörður on the east coast of Iceland. There are connections with Hanstholm in Denmark and Bergen in Norway, stopping at Lerwick in the Shetland Islands and Tórshavn in the Faroe Islands. From Hantsholm you spend two days in the Faroe Islands on the way there; from Bergen you spend two days in the Shetland Islands on the way back. **NorthLink Ferries**, **T** 0845-6000449, www.northlinkferries.co.uk, runs ferries from Aberdeen to Lerwick. The ferry are the only way to get your car or motorbike into the country but the journey is long and isn't any cheaper than flying.

Prices are given per person for a single journey to Iceland in high season, discounts are available in low season. From Hanstholm in Denmark (4½ days, €336, once weekly); from Bergen in Norway (48 hours, €224, once weekly); from Tórshavn in the Faroe Islands (15 hours, from €125, three times weekly); from Lerwick in the Shetland Islands (36 hours, £180, twice weekly); and from Aberdeen to Lerwick (12½ hours, £31.20).

Students receive a 25% discount with an ISIC card, groups of 15 or more get a 10% discount, children 6-15 go half price and under 6s free. From Seyðisfjörður Route 1 will take you to Reykjavík, 682 km away.

Getting around

Air
Air Iceland/Flugfélag Íslands, **T** 570 3030, www.airiceland.is, flies from Reykjavík City Airport to Akureyri (see p104).
Westman Islands Airline/Flugfélag Vestmannaeyjar, **T** 481 3255, www.eyjaflug.is, flies to Heimaey from Reykjavík and from the south-coast town of Bakki (see p99).

Bus
Around the city The yellow **Strætó** buses operate Monday to Friday 0700-2400, Saturday and Sunday 1000-2400. They are very reliable, running every 20 minutes around town before 1900 during the week and a little less frequently at weekends. Fares cost ISK 220, no change given. Lækjartorg Square is the main bus terminal where you can pick up route maps and timetables. Some night buses run until 0400. You get free bus travel with a Reykjavík Tourist Card.

Around the island The bus service is reliable, if not as regular as you might want, and it is possible to circumnavigate Iceland with a **Full Circle Passport** which allows you to travel in one direction around Iceland for ISK 38,800, with no time restrictions. A bus passport including the Western Fjords costs ISK 43,800. Check the timetables closely before you book as sections of roads may be closed when you're not expecting it. The departure point for all scheduled long-distance travel around Iceland is the **BSÍ coach terminal**, www.bsi.is, on Vatnsmýrarvegur (see Directory,

! The Romans talked about a place six days journey from Scotland which could conceivably have been Iceland. They called it Thule or Ultima Thule, now the name of a local beer. But there's no conclusive proof that they found the country. Just look at the roads.

Walking and cycling round the city

Tourist information centres have maps with walking and cycle trails marked. These are some of the best routes to take around town.

Around the Pearl
From the centre of Reykjavík, take the road along the Tjörnin beside the National Art Gallery, Fríkirkjuvegur, which turns into Sóleyjargata. Cross the main road at the end and head for Öskjuhlíð Hill with the shining Pearl at the top of it. Around the wooded area at the top and the bottom there are cycle trails which take you around the man-made geyser and forest area and down to the geothermal beach. From the beach you can take the trails either way along the sea towards Kópavogur or the more deserted peninsula beyond the airport.

Sea road
From the old harbour, follow the cycle trails east around to the statue of the Viking boat. From here you have a great view of Mount Esja and Engey and Viðey islands. If you've got a lot of energy, you can easily reach the Laugardalur Valley from here, and the botanical garden and thermal swimming pool; keep going and you'll find the new harbour and the ferry across to Viðey.

Grótta Beach
From the centre of Reykjavík, ride out towards the old harbour and take the road parallel to it, Vesturgata, a quiet and colourful residential street, until it reaches the sea at the end. Then follow the cycle path around to the east beside the coast where you'll see lots of seabirds. Keep going and you'll reach a wide beach and lonely lighthouse at its tip. It takes about an hour by bike to reach this unvisited spot with views far out to sea and a few frames for drying fish away from the residential areas.

p218). Bus passports can be bought from **Destination Iceland** at the BSÍ coach terminal, the Youth Hostel at Sundlaugavegur 34, **T** 553 8110, www.hostel.is, and the various bus terminals and tourist information centres around Iceland.

Car

There is only one real road around Iceland, the Route 1 or ring road that circles the island. It's mainly sealed, but can descend into a dirt track at times. Much of the interior is a barren desert wasteland, moon-like but without any discernable beauty, more like a giant mud field than a lava patch. Mobile phone signals cannot always be picked up outside residential areas, and if you were to find yourself stranded while driving through the interior you would need to be very lucky to get out safely. It's uninhabited for a reason and there aren't many passers-by. Travellers going alone can use the tourist notification number **T** 570 5900 to keep in touch. Travel in the central highlands of Iceland isn't a regular occurrence, mainly because the roads are only passable in the summer in these regions. Most roads open around mid-June although some as late as the middle of July and dates change according to snow cover and the spring melt, so you should contact the tourist information centre for further details. Up-to-date information about Iceland's roads including the mountain roads is available on **T** 1777.

Take a good map with you as well as a map of the nearest petrol stations and stay on the main road as far as possible. Be careful with bridges which often only allow one car at a time, and blind summits are common so care is needed. They are marked with a yellow sign saying *blindhæð*.

Car hire starts at around ISK 6400 per day for a small car including insurance and ISK 9900 for 4WD. Many companies can deliver cars to your guesthouse or hotel but if you want to hire a car from the airport you need to book in advance. For a list of agencies, see Directory, p212. For further information about driving in Iceland see www.vegagerdin.is.

Cycling

Reykjavík is suited to cycling as it is mainly flat. Bike rental is available from a number of places across town as well as a few guesthouses for around ISK 1700 a day, see p212. The **Icelandic Mountain Bike Club**, T 562 0099, www.mmedia.is/~ifhk/tourist.htm, offers advice on cycling around the country.

Ferry

Eyfar, Austurvegur 3, 630 Hrísey, T 462 7733, www.eyfar.is/enska.htm, runs the *Sævar* ferry between Hrísey and Árskógssandur, 35 km north of Akureyri (see p110).

Herjólfur, T 481 2800, www.herjolfur.is, runs ferries between Þorlákshöfn and Heimaey, the only inhabited island of the Westman Islands (see p99).

Seatours, Smidjustigur 3, 340 Stykkishólmur, T 438 1450, www.seatours.is, operates the *Baldur* car ferry across Breiðafjörður Bay between Stykkishólmur on the Snæfellsnes Peninsula and Brjánslækur in the Western Fjords (see p92).

Sæfari, Kjalarvogur, 104 Reykjavík, T 458 8000, www.samskip.com, runs ferries between Grímsey and Dalvík (see p104).

Taxi

Taxis charge uniform fares and tipping is not expected. Expect to pay around ISK 1000 for a 3 km journey; prices are higher in the evenings and at weekends. There's a taxi rank on Aðalstræti. For some taxi firm phone numbers, see p217.

Walking

The city is easy to walk around and has some nice coastal trails. A stroll around town won't take you longer than 20 minutes, although if you plan to visit places a little further afield like Árbær and Elliðaár Valley the bus ride takes 25 minutes from the central bus station at Lækjartorg Square. Laugardalur Valley is a 40-minute walk or a 10-minute bus ride away, and the Pearl and Nauthólsvík Beach

Reykjavík Tourist Card

If you're in Reykjavík for a limited amount of time, the **Reykjavík Tourist Card** is an economical way of seeing the major museums and swimming pools as well as being a free bus pass. It costs ISK 1200 for 24 hours, ISK 1700 for 48 hours and ISK 2200 for 72 hours, and can be bought at the tourist information centre, YHA, City Hall, *Mál og Menning* bookshops and BSÍ bus terminal.

are about a seven-minute bus ride from the centre, or a 30-minute walk. As yet, there are no walking tours of the city. However, it's not difficult to find your way about in the city and street names are clearly marked. Generally, sights are located by street name and not by street number because there is no need for more detail.

Tours

There are a huge number of trips you can take from Reykjavík into the interior, either in a group or by hire car. Some of them come with CD guides so you're not missing out on the spiel. Other more specialist trips require either experienced guides or nerves of steel on the unsurfaced roads. Tours are busy in the high season (June to September) and are informative and interesting. The best manage not to make you feel too much like a herd of sheep in the way that organized coach tours can. You will get the occasional stop at tourist shops though, but that's to be expected. For more specialized tours, including Icelandic pony trekking, see Sports, p195.

General tours
Adventure Center, **T** 1-800-228-8747 (USA), www.adventure center.com. Takes small groups from English speaking countries. Tours include family trips, trekking and cycling.

Discover The World, **T** 01737-218801 (UK), www.discover-the-world.co.uk/Iceland, offers year round, offers good-value year-round packages to Iceland and Greenland. Themed trips include Northern Lights tours, nature breaks and activities such as whale watching and husky sledging. There are also fly-drive packages and organised tours across the country, and particularly good deals with upmarket hotels like the *Borg* and *Óðinsvé* (see p116).

Icelandair Holidays, **T** 0870-7874020 (UK), www.iceland air.co.uk, offers weekend and longer breaks in Iceland staying at various top-rated hotels across Reykjavík from £289 for two nights including flights and taxes, November to March. They also offer themed breaks, hotel deals and car hire, see their website for details. Prices drop significantly in winter.

Icelandic Farm Holidays, **T** 570 2700, www.farmholidays.is. An association of farmers offering accommodation to travellers in their homes, guesthouses, and cottages throughout Iceland. Activities can include fishing, hunting, sailing, swimming, glacier tours and golf. Self-drive packages also available.

Iceland Saga Travel, **T** 1-508-825-9292 (USA), www.iceland sagatravel.com, offers escorted tours and customized itineraries.

Regent Holidays, **T** 0870-499 0437 (UK), www.regent-holidays.co.uk, has 30 years experience of running tours to Iceland and Greenland. Group tours or tailor-made itineraries available.

Air tours
Eagle Air, **T** 562 4200, www.eagleair.is. Offers sightseeing tours anywhere in Iceland in aircraft for up to nine passengers. It's an excellent way to appreciate the Icelandic landscape. Fly over glaciers, volcanos, waterfalls and geysers, or take a trip to see the midnight sun. A 1½-hour trip costs around ISK 15,500.

Bus tours

From Reykjavík Iceland Excursions, Funahöfði 17, 110 Reykjavík, **T** 540 1313, www.icelandexcursions.is. Year-round tours taking you as far afield as you can go in one day, including the central highlands, Hekla and Snæfellsness. Winter, Viking, caving and Northern Lights tours are also possible. The Golden Circle tour costs from ISK 6200.

Reykjavík Excursions, Vesturvör 6, 200 Kópavogur, **T** 580 5400, www.re.is. A similar range of year-round tours taking in many of the sights in a day from as far afield as Snæfellsness and Landmannalaugar to closer stops at the Blue Lagoon and the south coast. Horse riding, whale-watching and snowmobiling tours can also be arranged. A Golden Circle tour costs ISK 6800.

To Landmannalaugar Destination Iceland, **T** 585 4270, www.dice.is. Offers a self-guided trekking package costing around ISK 16,800 with mountain bus transport to Landmannalaugar, sleeping-bag accommodation and a map of the area.

Around Heimaey Viking tours, **T** 488 4884, www.boattours.is. Tours of Heimaey in minibuses or around the island by boat. Both cost around ISK 2000.

From Akureyri SBA Norðurleið, Hafnarstræti 82, 600 Akureyri, **T** 550 0700, www.sba.is. Bus tours from Akureyri around Mývatn and the local scenery. If you haven't much time to spare and want an authoritative guide, this is a good option, especially as it doesn't cost too much more than public transport.

Eldá Tourist Centre, 660 Mývatn, **T** 464 4220, www.elda.is. Runs minibus day tours and organized walks of Mývatn, and Jökulsá Canyon National Park. Tours run from June to September leaving at 0815 from Reykjahlíð with a minimum of three passengers.

Boat tours
Seatours, Smiðjustígur 3, 340 Stykkishólmur, **T** 438 1450, www.seatours.is. Boat tours from Smiðjustígur into Breiðafjörður fjord on the Snæfellsnes Peninsula (see p92). Tours run daily from May to September, and on request from October to April.

City and cultural tours
City Sightseeing, **T** 562 1011, www.city-sightseeing.is. 1 May - 15 Sep, departures every hour 1000-1600. ISK 1500, children ISK 750, under 11s free. Hop on-hop off bus tour which takes in the main sights and provides a recorded commentary. A convenient way to get to the main sights and rest your legs for a while. The ticket offers discounts for many of the sights.

Menningarfylgd Birnu, **T** 862 8031, www.birna.is. Walking tours of the city with a difference. The aim is to introduce visitors to the Icelandic history and culture by visiting unusual and quirky places. Tours can be tailored to specific requests. ISK 4000 per person.

Glacier tours
For activities on the glaciers you need to be with a guide and to have the correct equipment. The following tour operators cover the area around the capital and also offer more adventurous excursions. See also glacier hiking, p194.

Activity Group, Tunguháls 8, 110 Reykjavík, **T** 580 9900, www.activity.is. Operates super jeep tours combined with activities such as snowmobiling or dog sledding on a glacier. Offers day tours as well as longer trips. Recommended.

Iceland Rovers, Storhöfði 15, 110 Reykjavík, **T** 567 1720, www.icelandrovers.is. Land Rover tours taking in the Northern Lights in winter and Langjökull glacier, Landmannalaugar and Þorsmörk all year round, plus tailor-made tours.

Mountain Taxi Adventure Jeep Tours, **T** 544-5252,
www.mountain-taxi.com. Excellent tour company with 4WD jeeps
taking small groups on adventure tours of glaciers, Hekla and
Landmannalaugar, including some snowmobiling plus tailor-made
activity tours. Highly recommended experienced and entertaining
guides. A nine-hour trip to Landmannalaugar costs around
ISK 15,000 per person.

Hidden People tours
Guided Hidden World Tours, in Hafnarfjörður,
sibbak@simnet.is. Monday to Friday at 1000 and 1400 between
May and September. Tours around the lava to find 'the hidden
people' with an experienced English-speaking all-seeing guide
cost ISK 1700 per person and you need to book.

Whale-watching tours
From Reykjavík   Elding, **T** 555 3565, www.elding.is. Trips at
0900, 1300 and 1700, and midnight sun cruises which can be
arranged later into the evening. Also offers fishing, jet-ski and
Puffin Island cruises and have another boat running out of Keflavík.
Two-hour trips to Lundey cost ISK 2500. Trips leave from Keflavík
Harbour five times a day (May to September) with a coach pick-up
in Reykjavík and can take you further south where you're more
likely to see orcas. You get a free trip if you don't spot anything.

Iceland Travel, Lágmúli 4, 128 Reykjavík , **T** 585 4300. Amongst
other activities, offers four-hour whale-watching trips from April to
September, departing twice daily, and cost around ISK 3500.
Transfers can be arranged from your hotel.

Whale Watching Centre, **T** 533 2660, www.whalewatching.is.
Boats sail at 0900 and 1300 daily June to August. ISK 3800, ISK 1500
children. You can be picked up at your hotel for an additional ISK 500
if you don't fancy the walk or taking the bus. You'll be taken out into

→ Weather to go

	Sunrise	Sunset	Av temperature max/min	
			°C	°F
May	0355	2212	7/2	44/9
June	0242	2332	13/1	55/6
July	0323	2300	15/2	59/4
August	0458	2122	13/3	55/9
September	0629	1933	13/0	55/4
October	0755	1748	6/1	43/0

Faxaflói Bay with a view of Snæfellsjökull, Akranes and the steam from the Blue Lagoon on a good day. Typically you might see minke whales and dolphins as well as the occasional blue whale, and if you don't see anything you get a ticket for a free trip another day. A round trip is three hours long and takes in Lundey (Puffin Island) on the way back. This is the only place in Reykjavík where you'll see a puffin, apart from in a restaurant. There are around 10,000 breeding pairs on this tiny island alone.

From Húsavík North Sailing, Gamli Baukur, 640 Húsavík, **T** 464 2350, www.northsailing.is. ISK 3600, children 7-14 ISK 1800, under 7s free. The older of the Húsavík companies, making three- hour tours of the bay on a wooden-hulled former herring boat and a former shark-hunting boat. Trips run at 1330 daily year round, and up to four times a day June-August.

Gentle Giants, Harbourside, 640 Húsavík, **T** 464 1500, www.gentlegiants.is. Adults ISK 3000. Runs three hour tours of the bay in an oak hulled boat. They also run once daily year round at 1300, and up to four times a day June to August. Additionally from 15 June-15 July midnight sun tours from 2330.

Tourist information

The Centre, Aðalstraeti 2, 101 Reykjavík, **T** 590 1500, www.visit reykjavik.is. *Jun-Aug daily 0830-1800, Sep-May Mon-Fri 0900-1700, Sat-Sun 1000-1400*. The main tourist information centre with a wealth of information about the country as a whole as well as Greenland and the Faroe Islands. They can arrange tours, car hire, concert tickets and just about everything else you could want as well as information on daily events and nightlife. There is also a bureau de change inside the building and you can claim your tax refund here so that you have time to spend it before you get to the airport. Comprehensive website.

Iceland Visitor, Lækjargata 2, 101 Reykjavík, **T** 511 2442, www.icelandvisitor.is. *1 Jun-31 Aug, daily 0900-2200, 1 Sep-31 May, Mon- Sat 1000-1800*. Local travel agency offering information and booking service on a wide selection of tours, holiday packages, car rentals and accommodation.

This is Iceland, Laugavegur 20, 101 Reykjavík, **T** 561 6010, www.this.is/iceland. A friendly and helpful information centre offering free internet and free tour booking service, as well as plenty of information about the country and city. It's easy to spot, on the main street, with a red canoe across the front wall. They can help you out with customized tours, activities, car rental and accommodation.

Hafnarfjörður   Hafnarfjörður Tourist Information Center, Town Hall, Strandgata 6, 220 Reykjavík, **T** 585 5500, www.hafnarfjordur.is. *Mon-Fri 0800-1700, Jun-Aug also open Sat-Sun 1000-1500*. Very helpful and friendly tourist centre with information, accommodation booking service and maps of Hidden Worlds. Book your elf-spotting tour here.

Useful web resources

www.goiceland.org North American Tourist Board
www.icelandreview.is Daily magazine, also available online
www.visitreykjavik.is Icelandic Tourist Board
www.rvk.is Useful information about Reykjavík
www.whatson.is Festivals and events
www.simaskra.is Online phone directory for business and people

Westman Islands Básaskersbryggja, 900 Vestmannaeyjar,
T 481 3555, www.eyjar.is/eyjar. *Mon-Fri 0800-1700, Sat-Sun 1100-
1600*. Friendly tourist office in the ferry terminal building, with full
information on the island plus the legendary annual festival
(see p99) and wildlife.

Akureyri Hafnarstræti 82, Akureyri, **T** 462 7733, www.eyjafjordur.is.
*Jun-Sep Mon-Fri 0730-2030, Sat-Sun 0800-1700, Oct-May Mon-Fri
0800-1700, closed weekends*. Beside the bus station. Provides
information about the region including bus tours and other
transport and hotel availability. They can book accommodation
and also have information about kayaking or sailing in the fjord.

Maps
The tourist information centre provides a wealth of free maps and
guides to the city. The best of these is the yellow *Information For
Tourists* guide and the *City of Reykjavík* fold-up map that has a
street index, bus routes and timetables. Landmælingar Íslands
and Mál og Menning produce the best maps of Iceland. They are
expensive but are worth buying in Iceland rather than bringing
any of the less detailed foldout maps available abroad, particularly
because the roads are less than predictable and often greater
detail is needed. These maps also mark out smaller sights of
natural interest that are otherwise easily missed.

101 Reykjavík 39 This hip and happening postal district gave its name to an art-house movie. It covers the old town and includes the Alþing parliament building, town pond and City Hall, National Museum, Árni Magnusson Institute and the stunning Hallgrímskirkja church.

Old Harbour 54 There's something fishy about this otherwise charming part of 101, where you'll find the excellent Harbour House Museum and some interesting walks.

Laugardalur Valley 60 The city's sports centre also has natural hot springs, botanical gardens and the Ásmunder Sveinsson Sculpture Museum and garden.

Öskjuhlíð Hill 64 This city icon is topped by the outlandish Pearl and comes with its own fake geyser and centrally heated beach.

Elliðaár Valley 70 Site of the oldest recorded meeting point for Icelandic settlers, with the outstanding Árbær Museum and Árbæjarlaug thermal pool, boasting the finest view of all the city's pools.

101 Reykjavík

101 is both the oldest and the hippest part of town. Not too long ago, Reykjavíkurs were moving away to the outskirts, but now the trend is being reversed. It's the main area for restaurants, bars and shopping in the centre of the city and has colourful corrugated-iron clad houses, museums and the town pond. The sights are worth exploring and the walk along the harbour is beautiful. Alternatively, you can soak up the atmosphere of the city in the small cafés and hot pots of Reykjavík's seven swimming pools.

▸▸ *See Sleeping p115, Eating and drinking p140, Bars and clubs p159*

Sights

Lækjatorg Square
Map 2, D3, p250

Lækjatorg Square is the centre of the city from where the roads radiate. It's not a pretty place but houses the main bus station and will help you to orientate yourself. Opposite the square you'll see a proud, striding Viking on the top of a grassy hill. That's Ingólfur Arnarson, the city's first settler who reached Iceland in AD 874.

● *The hill, Arnarhóll, is a good viewpoint for occasional concerts held here in the summer. The buildings behind it are the Supreme Court, the Ministry of Finance and the National Theatre.*

Austurvöllur Square
Map 2, E3, p250

Although Lækjartorg Square is the centre of the city, this is the real heart of the city. The name means 'east field' and was originally at least six times bigger than it is today. Farmers riding into the city for business left their horses at Lækjartorg Square to camp in the

The people who went to Iceland were the Vikings. And they went because they couldn't deal with authority in Norway. So they flew off into this mad ocean in a wooden boat which is pretty hardcore, North Atlantic in the year 800. And found this island full of snow. Yeaah!

Björk (Q magazine May 1994)

area. Today, it's still a grassy square, in front of the Alþing (Parliament House), surrounded by bars and cafés and overlooked by the rather stern-looking statue of Jón Sigurdsson. He's a national hero, a politician who led the 19th-century movement towards independence from Denmark. When it finally came in 1944, it was decided that his birthday, 17 June, should be celebrated as the National Day. In the corner of the square is a small church, which is actually the city cathedral, built 1787-1796 and enlarged in the mid-18th century. It's not as grand or forbidding as Hallgrímskirkja on the hill above the city but is nevertheless an important ecclesiastical building.

Also in the square is *Hotel Borg*, a graceful white art-deco hotel overlooking the square (see p116). This was Iceland's first luxury hotel and deserves a look round for the architecture, well-preserved rooms and sense of grandeur. You can see why Marlene Dietrich stayed here in 1944.

● *Only slightly less likely is the fact that the Icelandic rock revolution of the 1980s began here, when New-wave music took hold and the hotel became a mecca for the city's young punks.*

Aðalstræti
Map 2, D2/3, p250

This is the oldest street in Reykjavík and houses the city's main tourist information centre, see p35. On the corner, underneath the new *Hotel Centrum*, is the site of an archaeological dig where the impressive remains of a Viking longhouse from the Settlement Period (AD 874-930) have been found. It's been mooted that this was the farmstead of Ingólfur Arnarson and is certainly one of the earliest settler houses. The site is due to open as a museum in 2006, www.citymuseum.is, and will contain exhibitions and multimedia displays about the life of the people and animals that lived in Reykjavík at that time.

Heart of the city
Austurvöllur Square has always been an important meeting place for Reykjavíkurs and today its grassy centre still attracts city folk.

This area was where weaving, the first industry in Reykjavík, began under the gaze of Skúli Magnússon. His statue stands just opposite, a heavy-browed, serious-looking man. In 1749 he worked to change the manor farm estate into a seat of industry with wool-processing factories and workers' cottages all along Aðalstræti. On the right-hand side of the street here is an old well which used to be one of the city's main water sources. The city's oldest surviving house is at Aðalstræti 10, dating from 1752.

Tjörnin
Map 2, E2/F2/G2, p250 and p251

The town pond, Tjörnin, is popular with young and old alike and frequently has a cluster of children round it feeding the ducks and greylag geese. It freezes in winter and people used to skate on it before the ice rink was built. It was created millions of years ago at the end of the last ice age as a sand and gravel bar was built up by the pounding waves of Faxaflói Bay.

● *Across Tjörnin you can see the street of Tjarnargata with its distinguished early 20th-century timber houses.*

City Hall (Ráðhús)
Year round Mon-Fri 0800-1900, Sat-Sun 1200-1800. Free. Café daily 1200-1330, snacks from around ISK 600. Map 2, E2, p250

The modern building, which seems to rise out of the water, was designed in 1987 as the result of a national competition. It stands right on the edge of the pond with a footbridge leading across into it. Inside, the second and third floors are reserved for the city council who meet here on the first and third Thursday of each month, but the first floor is open for visitors and is designed to be an extension of the streets outside. Here you'll find a large relief map of Iceland, a small tourist information centre and a café serving drinks, soup and sandwiches.

National Gallery of Iceland (Listasafn)
Fríkirkjuvegur 7, east side of the pond, **T** 515 9620, www.listasafn.is. *Year round Tue-Sun 1100-1700. Guided tours Sun 1500 and Tue 1240. ISK 400, children under 12 free, free on Wed. Map 2, G3, p251*

The National Gallery has a vast collection of art but the lack of space means only a limited amount of pieces can be displayed. It contains works by many of the significant Icelandic artists such as Érro, Einar Hákonarson, Jón Stefánsson, Guðmundur Þorsteinsson and a significant collection by Ásgrímur Jónsson. However, it doesn't have the range that you might expect – you really have to go to Kjarvalsstaðir or the Harbour House for that. It shows a variety of touring exhibits from all over the world, has a small sculpture garden and is one of the only places displaying paintings and sculptures from the 19th as well as 20th century. The building itself was built as a freezing plant in 1920 and later became one of Reykjavík's most popular danceclubs before it burnt down in 1971. In 1988 it was restored and became the nation's art gallery. The garden here holds a number of interesting statues speaking volumes about Icelandic society – *The Footballman*, *The Viking* and *The Girl* being three of them.

Old Graveyard
Map 2, F1, p250

Across the pond, on Suðurgata, just off Tjarnargata, the old graveyard is worth a wander round to give you an insight into the unusual patronymic naming system. You'll see a number of Viking-style memorials here, too, and there's a poetic, bohemian atmosphere about the place. Look out for the memorial to the father of the republic, Jón Sigurdsson, and Magnus Magnússon's grave. It's not the final resting place of the father of Mastermind though, and just goes to show that with a naming system such as this, it's not surprising that there are a few namesakes in this country!

● *At the top of the pond beyond the old graveyard you come to the university area. There are a few interesting museums up this way if you're interested in Nordic culture and the medieval sagas – Iceland's crown jewels.*

★ National Museum of Iceland
Suðurgata 41, **T** 530 2200, www.nationalmuseum.is. *1 May-15 Sep 1000-1700, 16 Sep-30 Apr 1100-1700, first Thu of each month until 2100, closed Mon. ISK 600, children free. Free on Wed. Shop and café. Map 1, F2, p248*

Re-opened in 2004 after extensive renovation, the National Museum takes you through 1200 years of Iceland's history, displaying the country's stunning Viking past and development

★ **Things in life for free**

Best

- Entry to the national parks
- Perlan city viewpoint, p64
- Swimming at Nauthólsvík Beach, p65
- Natural wonders of the Golden Circle, p84
- The Northern Lights, p102
- Coffee in many of the Laugavegur shops, p148

from the time of settlement to the present day. The museum's permanent exhibition 'The making of a nation' is conceived as a journey through time, beginning on a boat in which the medieval settlers crossed the ocean to their new home, and ending with an airport, the modern Icelanders' gateway to the world. The displays cover diverse aspects of the country's history and culture, including multimedia displays on topics such as mythology, the construction of early Viking buildings, the adoption of Christianity, the Reformation and the Census of 1703. Downstairs is Iceland´s largest public collection of images as well as temporary exhibitions. It is well worth a visit and the best place to gain an insight into how the nation has developed.

Nordic House (Norræna Húsið)
Sturlugata 5, **T** 551 7030, www.nordice.is. *Exhibition rooms Tue-Sun 1200-1700, closed Mon. ISK 300. Library daily 1200-1700. Free. Map 2, K1, p251*

This represents something of a cultural link between Iceland and other Nordic countries, with a library of modern Scandinavian literature, a café and an exhibition hall. The building was designed by contemporary Finnish architect, Alvar Aalto, and is very modern and unusual in design. Classical concerts are often held here.

Talk on water
Reykjavik's City Hall, where the politicians debate local issues, seems to rise out of the town pond.

▶ The naming police

It used to be law in Iceland that any foreigners wanting to settle permanently in the country had to change their name to the Icelandic patronymic style, attaching -son or -dóttir to the first name of their father. Things have relaxed these days, but Icelanders are still subject to certain rules when naming their children and occasionally immigrants with names that are difficult to pronounce or contain letters not in the Icelandic alphabet have to be renamed. Children's names must follow the Icelandic laws of possession, not be longer than three names and have some kind of history within the country. These complicated administrative laws caused a French immigrant with an unpronounceable name to rename himself Eilífur Friður, Icelandic words following the correct grammatical rules meaning 'eternal peace'.

National and University Library

Þjóðarbókhlaða, Árngrímsgata 3, 107 Reykjavík, **T** 525 5600, www.bok.hi.is. *Aug 20-May 20 Mon-Thu 0815-2200, Fri 0815-1900, Sat 1000-1700, Sun 1100-1700, May 21-Aug 19 Mon-Fri 0900-1700, Sat 1000-1400, closed Sun. Free. Map 1, F1, p248*

This huge red-and-white building is not actually within 101 but worth noting because it occasionally has small displays on contemporary cultural figures, like the Nobel-prize winning author Halldór Laxness. There are also email facilities here. Visitors are welcome to use the library which has a coffee bar on the second floor and a good range of books on Iceland.

 The Icelandic phone book lists people by their first name not their surname.

Bankastræti and Skolavörðustígur
Map 2, E4/F4/F5, p250

These streets, to the east of Austurvöllur Square and south of Lækjartorg Square, are characterized by a colourful array of corrugated-iron clad houses and shops dating from around 1910-1930. Bankastræti is one of the best places to begin your bar crawl in the evening, or alternatively somewhere to rest up in a café after a walk round town. There are also a number of good restaurants in this area to suit all budgets, from *Gott í Goggin* (see p150) to the highly rated *Siggi Hall* (see p144). The streets here are ideal for souvenir hunting, especially Skólavörðustigur with its small independent art galleries and craft shops.

★ Hallgrímskirkja
Skólavörðustígur, **T** 510 1000. *Daily 0900-1700. Suggested donation ISK 50, tower view ISK 350 adults, ISK 50 children.*
Map 2, H6, p251

This controversial, rugged ecclesiastical building, reminiscent of a volcanic eruption, was designed by state architect Guðjón Samúelson following a national competition to create a church for the hilltop to hold 1200 people with a 74-m-high tower that could double as a radio mast. Some 49 years in the making (1945-1986), it's as impressive inside as out and the steeple has the best view of the city by far. The church is named after the Reverend Hallgrímur Pétursson (1614-1675), the country's foremost hymn writer, whose hymns are still regularly sung today. Three co-ordinated bells in the tower are named after him, his wife Guðríður and his daughter Steinunn. The church holds services at 1100 on Sundays for its 7000 parishioners. It also holds occasional classical concerts.

★ **Quirky pieces of Icelandic design**

- Viking-style gravestones in the old graveyard, p44
- Hallgrímskirkja, p49
- Sólfar, Viking boat sculpture, p56
- Unusual paper clip-style public water fountains, p56
- Húsavík church, p112

Einar Jónsson Museum

Eiriksgata **T** 551 3797, www.skulptur.is. *1 Jun-15 Sep Tue-Sun 1400-1700, closed Mon. 16 Sep-31 May Sat-Sun 1400-1700, closed weekdays. Closed Dec-Jan. ISK 400, children under 16 free. Garden open year round, free.   Map 2, H6, p251*

Einar Jónsson (1874-1954), Iceland's first sculptor, was particularly influenced by religious and mythological themes. The museum stands adjacent to Hallgrímskirkja, where he chose to locate it. In his own words, "a desolate hill on the outskirts of town". Originally intended to be more of a cultural centre, it's certainly a nexus for tourist traffic with the imposing church so close. The museum is well worth a look if you like allegorical and classical sculpture.

ÁSI Art Museum

Freyjugata 41, **T** 511 5353, www.asi.is. *Year round Tue-Sun 1400-1800, closed Mon. Free.   Map 2, I7, p251*

Behind the church on Barónsstígur you'll find the city's only indoor swimming pool, Sundhöllin (see p198). At the other end of the road, where it interesects Freyjugata, is the ÁSI. This is the labour union's art gallery and shows mainly modern Icelandic and foreign art with frequently changing exhibits. One of the main draws is the building itself, an example of 1930s Icelandic functionalist style with a curved roof, and once the home of

Abstract expression
An example of the work of Ásmunder Sveinsson, one of the pioneers of modern Icelandic sculpture.

Ásmunder Sveinsson (1893-1982). You can see his sculptures in the Ásmunder Sveinsson Sculpture Museum in Laugardalur (see p62).

Kjarvalsstaðir (Reykjavík Art Museum)
Flókagata, 105 Reykjavík, **T** 517 1290, www.listasafnrey kjavikur.is.
Daily 1000-1700. ISK 500, ticket also includes entry to the Harbour House Museum (see p54) and Ásmunder Sveinsson Sculpture Museum (see p62) on the same day. Free on Mon.   Map 1, E5, p248

Not technically in 101 but a short walk from the ÁSI, this has the best range of Icelandic and foreign art. Don't be disappointed by the exterior of this gallery which seems a little concrete and uninspiring, inside is a welcoming and open space with contemporary international and Icelandic photography and artwork. Kjarvalsstaðir is named after the romantic and bohemian Icelandic artist Jóhannes S Kjarval (1885-1972) who donated many of his works and belongings to the city in 1968. Exhibitions from the Kjarval collection are regularly on display here; abstract renderings of Icelandic landscapes complete with personifications of the elements. Kjarval particularly enjoyed characterizing the way that colour changes in response to varying light, a particularly Icelandic characteristic of nature.

● *The museum grounds, Miklatún, are open for walks and there is a pleasant café.*

Culture House (Þjóðmenningarhúsið)

Hverfisgata 15, **T** 545 1400, www.thjodmenning.is. *Daily 1100-1700. Free tours in English at 1530 Jun-Aug weekdays (except Wed), Sep-May on Fri. ISK 300, free on Wed. Map 2, D5/E5, p250*

The colourful houses along Hverfisgata, some dating from the 19th wcentury, give a feeling of what it must have been like to live in the city in the past. The large, white Culture House (formely the city library) contains exibitions on the history and culture of Iceland, the country's independence and governance, as well as its ancient and modern literature. It contains the country's largest display of precious **medieval manuscripts**, which represent the cornerstone of Icelandic history, genealogy and culture and were collected by the Ární Magnússon Institute. The works are the richest evidence on the culture and mentalities of Northern Europeans in pagan times. They are displayed in near darkness to prevent any damage to the 1000-year-old calfskins on which they're written.

! Árni Magnússon (1663-1730), professor at the University of Copenhagen, recognized the importance of the manuscripts and sent many to Denmark to preserve them from Iceland's damp climate. Unfortunately many of them were destroyed in the Great Fire of Copenhagen. Those that survived were eventually returned to Iceland between 1971 and 1997.

> ### DIY surnames

Iceland retains the patronymic naming system which explains why to the untutored ear, all surnames sound the same. An Icelandic surname is made up of your father's first name, say Jón, plus either son – *son* – or daughter – *dóttir*. Any daughter of Jón will therefore be called Jónsdóttir and any son, Jónsson. Grandchildren often take their forenames from their grandparents which can make things even more complicated. It all sounds wonderfully exotic in Icelandic. If your dad's been blessed with the name Trevor things are all a little different.

Reykjavík

Bad Taste Gallery (Smekkleysa)

Laugavegur 59, in the basement, **T** 534-3730, www.smekkleysa.net. *Sun-Thu 1200-1800, Fri till 1900, Sat till 1700. Map 2, F8, p250*

Bad Taste is the record label that launched many of Iceland's best-known bands including Bjork, Sigur Rós, The Sugercubes, Reptile, Ham and Maus. The record shop and gallery has displays on the history of many Icelandic artists and the history of modern culture, while the popular 'Lobster or Fame' exhibition is a collage of the label's history including record sleeve designs, posters and photos.

Skuggi Gallery

Hverfisgata 39, **T** 511 1139, www.galleriskuggi.is. *Thu-Sun 1300-1700. Free. Map 2, F8, p250*

The Skuggi Gallery is a small family-run art space showcasing some of the quirkier aspects of Reykjavík's modern art scene. It's only large enough to show one exhibition at a time and displays a range of international and local artists' work. If it's an idiosyncratic look at local living and the natural scenery you're after, this is a good place to start.

Old Harbour

*Sundahöfn, the new harbour, has replaced the central harbour
around Sæbraut as the main centre for fishing vessels. The old
harbour has a certain charm though if you don't mind the lingering
smell of fish, and remains active with an influx of small fishing boats
every now and again. You can even see the old whaling boats,
marked 'Hvalur' across their bows, looking like they've seen better
days. At the weekend you can try some Icelandic delicacies at the
Kolaportið flea market.*

▸▸ *See Eating and drinking p152*

Sights

Harbour House Museum (Harfnarhús)

Tryggvagata 17, **T** 511 5155, www.listasafnreykjavikur.is. *Daily
1000-1700. ISK 500 joint ticket, see Kjarvalsstaðir, p51, children free,
free on Mon. Map 2, C2, p250*

This is part of the Reykjavík Art Museum (see p51) and houses
diverse exhibitions of work by Icelandic and foreign artists. The focus
is most definitely modern and experimental, with a permanent
exhibition by contemporary Icelandic artist Erró. He's famed in
Europe for his post-surrealist paintings, collages and narrative
paintings, many of which he donated to the city of Reykjavík in 1989.
They're a lot of fun and politically charged at the same time. Look
out particularly for his 'pope art' amid the pop art. The gallery also
has a café with a pleasant view of the harbour, and a small shop.

Kolaportið flea market

Geirsgata, **T** 562 5030. *Sat-Sun 1100-1700. Free. Map 2, C3, p250
See also Shopping, p188*

Harbour trips

From the top of the old harbour, at the opposite end from the Sólfar sculpture next to the old whalers, you'll find a couple of whale-watching tour boats in competition with the whalers. The best time to see whales in the Faxaflói Bay is July and August when they come to Iceland to teach their calves how to feed in the (slightly) warmer waters teeming with fish. Deep-sea fishing and jet-ski tours are also available, on demand. **Whale Watching Centre** is the bigger of the two operators, while **Elding** is smaller and a little more flexible

Held each weekend in the old customs building by the quay, you will find a host of stalls selling everything from bric-a-brac and second-hand clothing to a wide range of Icelandic books. There is also a good and cheap fish market.

● *If you've got adventurous taste buds and are prepared to feel queasy in the pursuit of the unusual, the Kolaportið market at the weekend has a fine array of fish, including putrefied shark meat in little cubes and harðfiskur, dried white cod. It tastes like fish-flavoured crisps and has a habit of getting stuck in your teeth.*

Reykjavík Maritime Museum (Víkin)

Grandagarði 8, **T** 517 9400, www.sjominjasafn.is. *Jun-Sep 1100-1700, closed Mon. ISK 500, children free. Map 2, D0, p250*

Situated in an old fish factory, with a great view over the harbour, the museum was opened in 2005 to celebrate the centennial of the first Icelandic trawlers and Reykjavík's age-old relationship with the sea. As a fishing and international shipping port, the entire Icelandic economy was long based upon the fisheries, and even today the ocean and its resources play a key role in Icelandic life. The museum focuses on maritime history and the fisheries over the centuries, presenting information through exhibits and models, as well as state-of-the-art video and computer technology. There are lots of plans for further development including a café, children's play area, and a reconstruction of the old harbour.

Reykjavík City Library

Tryggvagata 15, **T** 563 1750, www.borgarbokasafn.is. *Mon-Fri 1000- 2000, Wed 1100-1900, Sat-Sun 1300-1700; walking tours Jul-Aug Fri 1100, ISK 200 including a booklet on Icelandic literature and the city. Map 2, C2, p250*

The smaller of the city's libraries, with a café downstairs with comfy sofas and international newspapers. There are also bulletin boards for daily information and English books on the fifth floor. Internet access costs ISK 200 for half an hour downstairs; if you want an hour or longer it costs ISK 300 on the terminals on the fifth floor. You can also borrow CDs to listen to while you read.

Harbour walks

Walking east along the harbour on a clear day gives you fine views of Viðey Island with Mount Esja looming over it and the delicate scent of fish in the air. It's a very enjoyable 10-minute walk up to the Viking boat sculpture, past the fishermen with the catch of the day, but it can be windy and a little exposed. The sculpture itself, **Sólfar**, meaning 'Sun Voyager' points out towards sea and was made by Jón Gunnar Árnarson in 1971. It looks like it's floating on water itself, mounted on polished marble and gleaming silver against the sky.

Further along the harbour path is a bench where you can shelter a little from the wind and use the paper clip-shaped water fountain, its curves reminding you that Icelanders view art as a part of everyday life. Look across the main Sæbraut road back towards

Harbour highlights

The Harbour House Museum contains some of the country's best modern artworks, including the revered post-surrealist, Erró.

Smoke on the water

Reykjavík was settled in AD 877 by Norwegian Viking Ingólfur Arnarson. In true Viking style, Ingólfur heaved the posts of his high chair overboard and vowed that wherever they washed up he would settle.

Two years later his slaves found them washed up in an inlet seemingly full of smoke and the settlement was named 'smoky inlet', or Reykjavík. They later found the hot springs and saw that it was the steam that had made it look smoky.

Reykjavík today is still mainly smoke-free despite a growing number of cars, as geothermal energy keeps the city in everything from electricity to hot water. Excess hot water has even been used to heat a section of the North Atlantic so that Icelanders can relax at the beach without catching a chill. And the Vikings are celebrated by statues around the city as if it all had happened yesterday, some of the locals even being able to trace their ancestors back to Viking stock.

the city and you'll see Höfði, a cream-coloured wooden clapboard building. It's the reception house of the city council and hosted the momentous summit meeting of Reagan and Gorbachev in October 1986 which led to the end of the Cold War.

Walk in the other direction, or preferably take a bike, and you can reach the lighthouse on the edge of the **Seltjarnes Peninsula** and lonely **Grótta Beach**. The walk takes about two to three hours and runs right along the harbour's edge; bus No 3 also runs in this direction. Alternatively, walk the length of Vesturgata and when you reach the sea follow the path along the shore to the end. Grótta Beach itself is unspoilt, unlike Nauthólsvík Beach, and you can sit and watch the seabirds.

Modern art is rubbish?
It may look like a junkyard but the Harbour House Museum proudly exhibits many of the country's cutting edge artists.

Icelandic quirks

Best

- Belief in elves and ghosts
- Natural light fluctuations
- Under-pavement heating
- The hot tub on the beach
- Saying 'bless' for 'goodbye'

Laugardalur Valley

The name Reykjavík literally translates as 'smoky bay', as the first settlers mistook the steam from the hot springs in the Laugardalur Valley for smoke. This is the city's most important sports area, containing the National Indoor Stadium and football pitch as well as an Olympic-sized swimming pool and luxury spa complex. The springs are still used today in the comfortably warm pool and its various hot pots, as evidenced by the slight whiff of sulphur in the air.

▸▸ *See Sleeping p123, Sports p191*

◉ Sights

Laugardalslaug Thermal Pool and Spa

Sundlaugavegur 30a, 105 Reykjavík, **T** 553 4039. *Mon-Fri 0650-2130, Sat-Sun 0800-2000. ISK 200 adults, ISK 100 children. Spa,* **T** *553 0000, www.laugar.is. ISK 3500. Bus 14 from Lækjartorg Sq. Map 3, B8, p253*

This is the biggest of the city's seven thermal pools, attracting tourists and residents alike for the 50 m pool, slide, hot pots, steam room and sauna. See p198 for details on swimming etiquette.

Recently opened within the same complex is the city's most luxurious spa, with underground saunas and steam rooms of varying

Being able to play golf at midnight thanks to the 24-hour sunlight is one of the best things about being from Reykjavík. In contrast to London, it's a capital city where you can breathe fresh air when you're there. I always remember the feeling of driving around the town with views of the surrounding mountains everywhere you look. It always makes me feel at home and that's what I miss most when I'm away.

Eidur Gudjohnsen, Chelsea and Iceland footballer, September 2002.

themes, temperature, colour, humidity and aromas to help you completely unwind. For the full five-star treatment, you can indulge in a massage, mud-wrap or a glass of wine in the cosy, candelit bar.

Ásmunder Sveinsson Sculpture Museum (Ásmundarsafn)

Sigtún, 105 Reykjavík, **T** 553 2155, www.listasafnreykjavikur.is. *May-Sep daily 1000-1600, Oct-Apr 1300-1600. Part of the Reykjavík Art Museum, ISK 500 joint ticket, see Kjarvalsstaðir, p51, children free, free on Mon. Bus 14 from Lækjartorg Sq. Map 3, D7, p253*

Across the road from the sports complex you'll see an unusual white domed building surrounded by sculptures. It could almost be a space observatory, but is actually the former home and now museum of Ásmunder Sveinsson, one of the pioneers of Icelandic sculpture. Thirty of his abstract Henry Moore-like sculptures are displayed outside the building for free all year round, while inside the more delicate works are displayed, many of which draw on Icelandic literature, fairytales and nature. It's well worth a visit.

Sports complex

T 581 4444. *Map 3, C8, p253 See Sports, p191.*

The sports complex at Laugardalur comprises the football stadium, indoor sports hall and ice-skating rink. You can buy tickets for all events and find out about forthcoming games at the tourist information centre on Bankastræti. Football is only played in Iceland in the summer as it's both too dark and too wet to be played in the winter, so the stadium is well used in June to September for national and international men's and women's games. It's small by European standards though, seating only 7000 people. Handball is the main sport played in the indoor stadium.

Reykjavík Park and Zoo

Hafrafell v/ Engjaveg, 105 Reykjavík, **T** 575 7800, www.husdyragardur.is. *Daily 15 May-25 Aug 1000-1800, 26 Aug-14 May 1000-1700.12 years and over ISK 450, 5-12 years ISK 350, under 4s free. Bus 2, 10, 11, 12 or 15 from Lækjartorg Sq. Map 3, E9, p253.*

Behind the sports complex and next to the botanical garden, the park and zoo is only really exciting if you're under 12. The zoo contains farm animals, reindeer and mink and the park has a playground and boat rides on a pond. Recent additions include an aquarium and 'Science World'. See p207 for further details. There is also a restaurant on site.

Reykjavík Botanical Garden

Skúlatún 2, 105 Reykjavík, **T** 553 8870, botgard@rvk.is. *Daily Apr-Sep 1000-2200, Oct-Mar 1000-1700. Free. Bus 2, 10, 11, 12, 15. Map 3, E10, p253*

The botanical garden is a joy on a clear sunny day, with 2½ ha of good walking and cycling trails along the rock gardens, Japanese-style bridges, and Icelandic flora, such as it is. There's a small hothouse and café too. It's Reykjavík's answer to Central Park, though obviously on a much smaller scale, and is unusual in that it's one of the most wooded parts of the capital. There's an arboretum and a woodland area and this is one of the few places where the joke "What should you do if you get lost in an Icelandic forest? Stand up!" doesn't work. You can also see where the original hot springs were, where women used to cook, clean and make a kind of whey cheese, and the park is overlooked by the Áskirkja, a basalt church which looks like a ship's prow. The camping ground and youth hostel back onto the park (see p123).

Öskjuhlíð Hill

Dominated by the Pearl, Öskjuhlíð Hill was used by the British Army in the Second World War and has a number of walking and cycling trails around the hillside and down to the beach. Between the Pearl and the sea there's an artificial geyser which goes off roughly every five minutes and gives an idea of what lies in store at Geysir (see p87). The trees and shrubs could be said to constitute an Icelandic forest and it's worth exploring on foot, bike or rollerblades.

▸▸ *See Sleeping p126, Eating and drinking p153*

Sights

The Pearl (Perlan)
Öskjuhlíð, 105 Reykjavík, **T** 562 0200, www.perlan.is. *Observatory daily 1000-2330. Free. Café 1130-2200. Bus 13 from Lækjartorg Sq. Map 1, F5, p248*

Surrounded by pine trees, the Pearl is what James Bond's secret Icelandic headquarters should look like. Never mind that the latest epic *Die Another Day* was actually filmed on a glacial lagoon in the south of the country, or that the building is actually atop the city's hot-water storage tanks, Perlan is an amazing modern glass building with wonderful views across the city and out to sea. It became one of the city's iconic buildings when it opened in 1991 and art exhibitions, expos and concerts are regularly held here. The fourth floor has a small café with particularly good ice creams and a viewing deck. From here you can see out to the President's home of Bessastaðir as well as a volcanic ridge and the city airport. The fifth floor has an exceptional restaurant with a revolving floor that takes two hours to make a full circuit of the city and there's also a bar on the sixth floor.

★ Saga Museum

Öskjuhlíð, 105 Reykjavík, **T** 511 1517, www.sagamuseum.is. *Daily 1000-1800; winter 1200-1700. ISK 800, children ISK 400. Bus 13 from Lækjartorg Sq. Map 1, F5, p248*

Inside the Pearl on the ground floor is one of Iceland's finest museums, charting the early history of the country through the stories of the sagas. It's colourful, bloodthirsty and full of feuding Vikings, not to mention witches burned at the stake, and offers an excellent and highly recommended insight into Iceland's history and literature.

★ Nauthólsvík Beach

Follow the woodland trail down to the Ægisiða shore for about 7 mins and you'll find the man-made and very quirky Nauthólsvík Beach. Buses 3, 4 and 6 go to Ægisiða, and bus 5 goes to Skeljarnes for a shorter walk. Alternatively, take bus 7 to Perlan and walk down the hill. Free. Towels and showers provided. Map 1, H5, p248

Not only have they imported yellow sand here, as opposed to the naturally occurring black volcanic stuff, but there's a hot tub on the beach and the sea is pumped with geothermal water to keep it at a cool but bearable 10°C. Life doesn't get better than this – it's not just the Mediterraneans who get to hang out at the beach these days, you know. The locals even take the day off work to spend time at the beach. You've got to have a dip here, rain or shine, if only to say that you have. But if it's a nice day be warned – the beach is quite small and you might find yourself fighting for that last patch of man-made sand. There are changing rooms and a small, cheap café right on the beach as well as the turf-roofed *Kaffee Nauthóll*, a short walk away (see p153). The city is also trying to encourage roller-blading to take off amid the running and walking tracks along the coast.

The Pearl
Looking like some kind of futuristic space-pod, the Pearl is actually home to a museum about Iceland's origins, the Saga Museum.

▶ Whaling in Iceland

If you're prepared to have your ear bent for an hour or so, ask an Icelander what they think about whaling. As a political issue it's a bit of a hot potato to say the least. All whaling stopped in Iceland in 1989 following worldwide boycotts and economic pressure, which might go some way to explaining why in recent years the chance of spotting a whale in Icelandic water has risen to over 95%. Even when Iceland withdrew its membership of the International Whaling Committee (IWC) in 1999, it seemed unlikely that the country would take up the harpoon again as there was still an embargo on selling whale meat. But late in 2002 Iceland rejoined the IWC and was allowed to resume whaling for scientific purposes – much to the chagrin of foreign governments and environmental groups – and plans to resume commercial whaling from 2006.

Despite international criticism, 70% of Icelanders support the resumption of whaling. Many see it is as part of their cultural history and for centuries whales were a valuable food source and vital to their survival. The word *hvalreki* in Icelandic literally means 'beached whale' but has a more figurative translation these days as 'lucky find' or 'lottery win', harking back to when finding one would provide enough meat to last through a long, harsh winter. What's more, studies carried out by the Marine Research Institute (MRI) show that an abundance of whales can upset the food chain and have a negative impact on valuable fish stocks. However, as the country's dependence on tourism increases, it remains to be seen how the resumption of whaling will coexist with one of the country's fastest-growing industries – whale watching – and what effect this will have on Iceland's economy.

★ Things to do when it's raining

Best

- Check out the museums, p72
- Fly to Akureyri, p104
- Play backgammon in Kaffeebarinn, p161
- Lose yourself in a bookshop for an hour or so, p185
- Go swimming, p198

Sundahöfn and Viðey

The Viðey Island ferry, T 581 1010, www.ferja.is, runs 5 times daily from Sundahöfn, and once daily from Reykjavík city centre harbour. Return ticket ISK 750, children ISK 350. Map 1, A6, p248

To the northeast of the city, beyond Laugardalur Valley, Sundahöfn is the new harbour and has a ferry terminal taking day-trippers across to the small, historical island of Viðey, 3 km offshore. There are also a number of country walks around the area of Laugarnes, where you'll find a bizarre mismatched house with a pool table attached to its roof and free-standing sculptures in the garden. It belongs to Hrafn Gunnlaugsson, an Icelandic filmmaker both famed and reviled for his historical depictions of the Vikings as violent and primitive people.

Viðey was inhabited as early as the 10th century and the oldest stone building in Iceland was discovered there. The monastery, found during excavations, dates from the 13th century when it was the richest in the country. Following the Reformation in the 16th century, the island passed to the secular lords, then became a fishing community and is now inhabited by hundreds of birds who enjoy the rich grassland. There's a restaurant and a church and some lovely walks. Inside the old schoolhouse on the island you'll find a photographic exhibition about Viðey. Guided walks are offered in the summer and around the cliffs you'll see many thousands of seabirds. You can also see the nearby island of Lundey, home to tens of thousands of puffins.

69

Elliðaár Valley

The Elliðaár Valley, a 20-minute drive east of Reykjavík, is a lush green valley with a salmon river running through it, a thermal swimming pool, Reykjavík City Museum and, apparently, quite a few elves. The river is named after Elliði, the ship belonging to Ketillbjörn the Old from the town of Mosfell. There are a couple of historic sites here including Þingnes, south of the lake, thought to be one of the oldest places of assembly in Iceland. The fishing season runs from 15 June to 14 September. There are also a number of good hiking and biking trails in the area and some pony trekking tours head out this way. Contact the tourist information centre for further details.

▸▸ *See Sports p191, Tours, p29*

⊙ Sights

Árbær Museum (Árbæjarsafn)

Kistuhyl 4, 110 Reykjavík, **T** 577 1111, www.arbaejarsafn.is. *Jun-Aug Tue-Fri 1000-1700, Sat-Sun 1000-1800, Mon 1100-1600, Sep-May guided tours Mon, Wed, Fri 1300; otherwise by arrangement. Bus 110 from Lækjartorg Sq or bus 10 from Hlemmur. Map 1, D12, p249*

Árbæjarsafn is an open-air museum tracing the architecture and history of Reykjavík. Most of the houses originally come from the city centre with the oldest dating back to 1820. It's certainly an interesting peek into the past, showing clearly how the city has grown in the last 50 years, before which it was an oddment of houses scattered around the pond. Local actors dress up as workers from days gone by and there is an interesting collection of toys from the past. There's also a café in the midst of all the turf-roofed houses and it's a pleasant place to spend a sunny afternoon.

● *About a 15-20 minute walk from the museum along the river is the Árbæjarlaug outdoor swimming pool. It has a fantastic view and feels as though it's right in the countryside. See Swimming, p198.*

Reykjavík Tourist Card

Your key to the
Capital

The Reykjavík Tourist Card gives admission to all the thermal pools in Reykjavík, public transport, The National Museum, Reykjavík Art Museums, The National Gallery of Iceland, Reykjavík Zoo and Family Park, discount of tours and much more. The card is sold at The Centre, most Reykjavík hotels and other tourist centres. **Free Internet access for cardholders.**

Great value for money!

THE CENTRE
The Official Tourist Information Centre in Reykjavík
Aðalstræti 2 · 101 Reykjavík · Tel +354 590 1550
info@visitreykjavik.is · www.visitreykjavik.is

Reykjavík
PURE ENERGY

VISIT REYKJAVIK

Reykjavík

Northern street lights
When winter closes in on Reykjavík, it's not just a case of the nights drawing in, they almost take over. On a clear night though, you gain the chance to see the magical aurora borealis from the city itself.

Museums and galleries

• **Árbæjarsafn** (Arbaer Museum) Open-air architectural history of the city, p70.
• **Ásgrímur Jónsson Collection**, Bergstaðastræti 74, 101 Reykjavík, **T** 515 9600, www.listasafn.is. A department within the National Gallery of Iceland (see p43). Showcases the work of one of the country's lesser-known modern sculptors.
• **ASÍ Art Museum** Modern Icelandic and foreign art displayed in 1930s functionalist building, p50.
• **Ásmundur Sveinsson Sculpture Museum** Shows the delicate beauty of one of the pioneers of Icelandic scuplture, p62.
• **Bad Taste Gallery** Music store and gallery of Iceland's best-known record label, p53.
• **Culture House** Home to detailed accounts of Viking settlement and precious Saga manuscripts, p52.
• **Einar Jónsson Museum** Classical and allegorical sculpture, p50.
• **Harbour House Museum** Icelandic art, featuring a permanent exhibition by pop-art idol, Erró, p54.
• **Icelandic Institute of Natural History**, Hlemmur 5, 101 Reykjavík, **T** 590 0500, www.ni.is/english. *May-Aug Tue, Thu, Sat-Sun 1300-1700; Sep-Apr 1330-1600*. A collection of geological, botanical and zoological exhibits.
• **Kirsuberjatreð Gallery**, Vesturgata 4, 101 Reykjavík, **T** 562 8990, www.kirs.is. *Mon-Fri 1000-1800, Sat 1100-1500*. Beautiful old gallery run by 10 women artists known for their unusual approach and use of materials.
• **Kjarvalsstaðir** The best gallery in the city for Icelandic and foreign art, p51.
• **Living Art Museum** Vatnsstígur 3b, 101 Reykjavík, **T** 551 4350, www.nylo.is. *Wed-Sun 1300-1700*. Experimental art gallery.

Listings

Museums and galleries

- **Maritime Museum (Víkin)** A celebration of Iceland's important maritime history, see p55.
- **National Gallery of Iceland** 19th- and 20th-century Icelandic art and touring exhibitions, p43.
- **National Museum of Iceland** 1200 years of Icelandic history and culture displayed in all its fascinating glory, p44.
- **Nordic House** Cultural link to other Nordic countries, p45.
- **Numismatic Museum** Einholt 4, 105 Reykjavík, T 569 9962, www.sedlabanki.is. *Mon-Fri 0900-1700 or by arrangement.* A collection of coins and banknotes.
- **Reykjavík Electrical Museum** Rafstöðvarveg, Elliðaárdalur, 110 Reykjavík, T 516 6790, www.rafheimar.is. *Jun-Aug 1300-1700, Sep-May Sun 1500-1700 and on request.* History of the development of hydroelectric power production in Iceland.
- **Reykjavík Museum of Photography** Tryggvagata 15, 101 Reykjavík, T 563 1790, www.ljosmyndasafnreykjavikur.is. *Mon-Fri 1200-1900, Sat-Sun 1300-1700.*
- **Safn Gallery**, Laugavegur 37, T 561 8777, www.safn.is. *Wed-Sun 1400-1800.* Housed in a historic house, with displays of international and Icelandic contemporary conceptual art.
- **Saga Museum** Excellent insight into Iceland's culture and history, p65.
- **Sigurjón Ólafsson Museum** Laugarnestangi 70, 105 Reykjavík, T 553 2906, www.lso.is. *1 Jun-31 Aug Tue-Sun 1400-1700, 1 Sep-31 May Sat-Sun 1400-1700.* Modern sculpture.
- **Skuggi Gallery** Small and idiosyncratic modern art space, p53
- **Telecommunications Museum** Suðurgata, 101 Reykjavík, T 550 6410. *Year round Tue, Thu, Sun 1100-1700, also upon request.*

Around Reykjavik

Hafnarfjörður 77 Surrounded by lava fields and more elves than Tolkein would know what to do with.

Blue Lagoon 80 The country's top attraction where you can relax in 39°C healing water.

Golden Circle 84 The name given to a circular tour of Gullfoss waterfall, Geysir and the magnificent Þingvellir National Park.

Snæfellsnes Peninsula 92 The Snæfellsjökull Glacier is reputedly one of the world's strongest new-age energy fields.

Landmannalaugar 96 Mountains stained sulphurous yellow and sandstone orange and fields of shining obsidian chunks and rugged lava.

Vestmannaeyjar (Westman Islands) 99 A live volcano on Heimaey and an incredible amount of birdlife during the summer months.

Akureyri and around 103 Iceland's second-largest city is handily placed for outstanding scenery around Lake Mývatn and Húsavík, the best place in the world for whale watching.

Hafnarfjörður

*Known as 'the town in the lava', Hafnarfjörður (pronounced
Hab-nar-fyur-thur) is the most interesting of the city's suburbs. It's
only 10 km from the centre of Reykjavík and easy to reach by bus and
car. The town encircles the harbour, with lava fields around it, and is a
nice walking area. While you're there, look out for the elves, or 'hidden
people' – huldufólk – who, legend has it, live in the lava.*

*Hafnarfjörður is said to have the highest population of
otherworldly beings of any town in Iceland. This may be tourist hype,
too much brennivín or a trick of the light, but is nevertheless a good
enough reason to get out and enjoy the countryside. Eating and
drinking in this suburb doesn't compare to the city and the 10-minute
drive into Reykjavík is certainly worth it for the restaurants and
nightlife. The website www.hafnarfjordur.is is useful for information.*
▸▸ *See Sleeping p126, Eating and drinking p153, Tours p29*

*On Route 1 towards Keflavík. Bus S1 runs every 20 mins from
Lækjartorg Sq. The tourist information centre (see p35) provides
information about the area including 6 themed walks of the town and
a Hidden Worlds map, as well as booking accommodation and tours.*

◉ Sights

There are a number of scenic routes to take around the town, the
cliffs and the lava. The **Sculpture and Shore Walk** starts from the
tourist office on Vesturgata. Walk up the road away from the harbour
and down Herjólfsgata and along the coast. You get a great view of
Faxaflói Bay and the seabirds in the cliffs in the summer; watch out
also particularly for the *huldufólk* around Herjólfsgata. If you don't
see any, well, that's why they're called the 'hidden people'.

The **Elf Walk** begins where Hellisgata and Reykjavíkurvegur
meet. Walk to the Hellisgerði park which has a bonsai garden and is
home to a colony of elves. Then walk back down Reykjavíkurvegur

▶ **Away with the fairies**

"The stereotyped Icelandic person is someone who believes in elves and makes a concrete road that goes in a circle around an elf rock so not to upset them," so says Björk, the country's best-known spokesperson. It is a tradition that is particularly alive in Hafnarfjörður where a local seer has drawn a map depicting the best of the town's otherworldly dwellings. Other parts of Iceland have their own elf traditions and you might see the odd house painted on rocks as you drive around the south, to remind humans of the *huldufólk*.

There are apparently many different kind of beings to be found in the gardens of the town as they are particularly fond of the lava. There are the classic *álfar* – elves – who can be of many different sizes and shapes: the *huldufólk*, or 'hidden people', who look very much like humans and live together in social groups; the *ljúflingar*, 'lovelings', slender and graceful beings the size of ten year olds; temperamental *dvergar*, 'dwarves', about the size of toddlers and the amazing *tívar*, 'mountain spirits'. You'd certainly know if you saw one of these creatures, beautiful, bright and several hundred metres tall with a warmth radiating from them.

If you want to see them you have to be quiet and still and concentrate hard on feeling at one with your natural surroundings. In other words, show a little 'elf respect'.

and take a left down Hverfisgata. Some more elves live on the left-hand side of the road. Another good place to check out is to the top of Hellisgerði park at Nönnustígur where a several-hundred-year-old hermit lives. He's reputed to be friendly and relaxed.

The **Ástjörn Nature Reserve**, around the lake in the south of Hafnarfjörður, is a pleasant walk. Ásfjall is the smallest mountain

★ Best Places for spotting elves

- Elliðaár Valley, p70
- Hafnarfjörður, p77
- Þingvellir, p84
- Lake Mývatn, p106

in Iceland and is a good viewpoint over the harbour and surrounding area as well as into the lava and away to Helgafell in the other direction.

Viking Village (Fjörukráin)
Strandgata 50a, **T** 565 1213, www.fjorukrain.is. *Daily 1200-2200. Map 4, E3, p254*

Along the harbour from the tourist information centre you can see a strange looking wooden building with a carved dragon at its peak. This is the Fjörukráin Viking Village, a replica Viking hall and hotel serving up traditional feasts. The food, including lamb, schnapps and *skyr*, a thick yoghurty dessert, is exceptional and a banquet of traditional fare costs ISK 4600 including drinks and some great Viking and Valkyrie impersonations. It's worth peaking inside or stopping for a meal as it used to house the West Nordic Culture House and still contains some interesting artefacts.

Hafnarfjörður Museum
Vesturgata 8, **T** 585 5780, museum@hafnarfjordur.is. *Jun-Aug daily 1300-1700, Sep-May Sat-Sun 1300-1700. Map 4, D3, p254*

Hafnarfjörður Museum is housed in a renovated 19th-century warehouse and consists of a children's exhibition and a historical museum containing a number of texts, photographs and artefacts.

> ### The mystery of Lake Kleifarvatn

On the way to the Blue Lagoon you can take an alternative route out of Hafnarfjörður (Route 42 rather than 41), which will take you to another natural wonder. Lake Kleifarvatn used to be the deepest lake in Iceland, but geologists are puzzling over what's happened to it since the last major earthquake which caused the lake to drain away. No one quite knows where the water has gone or why. It looks like someone just pulled the plug out.

To the right of the lake as you drive along there's a geothermal area with bubbling mud pots and the occasional explosion. It's all a bit of a mystery, but legend has it that a snake-like monster the size of a whale lives in the water, which may explain it. The former lake is not far away from the city and a little off the main tourist route.

The museum also has two other houses on display: **Sívertsen House** (Vesturgata 6, Jun-Aug daily 1300-1700, Sep-May Sat-Sun 1300-1700) is the oldest house in Hafnarfjörður and has been restored to its original state. It's a good example of an upper-class home in the early 19th century. By contrast, **Sigga's House** (Kirkjuvegur 10, Jun-Aug Sat-Sun 1300-1700) is an example of a working-class home in the early 20th century.

★ Blue Lagoon (Bláa Lonið)

Just 40 minutes from the city and a popular stop on the way both to and from Keflavík Airport, the Blue Lagoon is one of Iceland's most visited tourist attractions. In a country with such an exuberance of outstanding beauty, this is high praise indeed – especially for what is essentially a lido.
▸▸ *See Sleeping p127, Map 6, E2, p256*

240 Grindavík, **T** 420 8800, www.bluelagoon.is. *15 May-31 Aug daily 0900-2100, 1 Sep-14 May daily 1000-2000. ISK 1400, children ISK 700. From Jun-Sep buses leave 6 times daily to the Blue Lagoon from the BSÍ bus station, ISK 1000 one way, and 3 times daily from Keflavík Airport, www.bustravel.is. By car, take Route 41 from Reykjavík towards Keflavík and then Route 43 to Grindavík. Reykjavík Excursions and Iceland Excursions (see p31) both offer tours and airport transfers.*

Situated next to the slightly disturbing Svartsengi power plant, the Blue Lagoon is a large splash of milky-blue water in the middle of an otherwise desolate volcanic landscape that makes use of the geothermal water passing through the plant. Overspill from the powerplant was pumped into the lava fields to drain away but minerals in the water crystallized, thus creating the pool used today. The colour might remind you of a chemical waste dump, but the distinctive hue actually comes from the minerals and blue-green algae that have dissolved into the seawater and which has been proved to have a positive effect on the skin.

The temperature is kept at 36-39°C all year round and gives you a nice fuzzy warm feeling. The bottom of the pool is mainly sand, although at the far corners you'll find some silica mud in pots, especially good for healing skin complaints. Massages and beauty treatments are available at the pool, book in advance. Make sure that you follow the correct swimming pool procedure (see p198) and remember to bring some shampoo, conditioner and moisturiser, as the salt water leaves you feeling dry and matted if you don't wash your hair a good few times afterwards. You can hire swimming costumes and towels if you forget to bring them with you. It's good value for money (for Iceland) and well worth a visit. There's also a snack bar and seafood restaurant which looks out onto the surreal landscape.

Deep Blue
The milky blue waters surrounded by lava are great for a dip at any time of the year.

Golden Circle

The Golden Circle is the highly publicized circular tour of three of Iceland's finest natural and historic features within a day's journey of Reykjavík. Starting at Þingvellir National Park, the ancient site of the Viking parliament you can then take in Geysir and Strókkur, two spouting geysers, and finish at the highlight, Gullfoss, the Golden Falls, so-named because of the rich rainbow colours you can see as sunlight shines through the mist. The sights are equally worth seeing individually, especially Þingvellir where you could spend a few days walking around the dramatic scenery.

▸▸ *See Sleeping p128, Tours, p29*

Sights

★ Þingvellir National Park

T 482 2660, www.thingvellir.is. *Daily 1 May- 30 Sep until 2200, café 1 Apr- 31 Oct, 1 Nov- 31 Mar weekends only. Free. Þingvellir Service Centre has information and sells fishing and camping permits. 49 km northwest of Reykjavík it is easily reached by taking Route 1 out of the city towards Mosfellsbær and then Route 36 from which it is signposted. From 24 May to the end of Aug buses to Þingvellir go once daily at 1330 from the BSÍ bus station and return once daily from Valhöll in Þingvellir at 1645. They cost ISK 1020. Map 6, E3, p256*

One of Iceland's most visited sights, Þingvellir (pronounced Thingvellir), is blessed with an active rift landscape and a remarkable history (see box, p85). More remarkable though is that much of the park is a kind of no-man's-land. Look around as you enter the park and you can see a dramatic rift in the earth, in the shape of dark cliffs rising up from the grassland. This is the American tectonic plate tearing away from the Eurasian plate, moving apart at an average of 2 cm each year. Further across the park you can see the same kind of scar in the opposite hill – the Eurasian plate. What is left in the

Getting together

The Vikings chose Þingvellir as the site of their assembly, the Alþing (Þingvellir means 'parliament fields') because it was easily reached from all the settlements, albeit a few days on horseback for some. The first parliament, or meeting, was held here in AD 930, making it the oldest recorded general assembly in the world.

Chieftains, or *goðar*, from district assemblies convened to formally settle disputes. During the two weeks of the assembly people gathered from miles around to trade, exchange news and look for work and it was the one time when the inhabitants of the small, lonely farmsteads came together as a nation.

middle is new land created between the two, neither American nor European. Iceland is often left off the European map, to many an Icelanders' chagrin, has rejected membership of the EU and is certainly not about to become a lone state of America. It is poetically symbolic that the country straddles the two continents and is forging a new land all of its own.

The Viking assembly site was at **Lögberg**, or **Law Rock**, from AD 930 until 1271, and this is where a lot of coach parties stop. From the tourist information centre, take the road down towards the church and small farm building until you reach the car park. The Lögberg is marked with a flag on the right-hand side of the river. It's a natural platform for speeches and the speaker could be seen and heard from some distance around. Anyone attending the assembly had the right to ask for help on any issue from the Law Rock, where discussions began at 1800 on each day of the parliament. All issues were settled in one sitting and generally money changed hands to find a resolution. From here you can look out over the river and **Lake Þingvallavatn**, with the high wall of the Almannagjá fault, the American plate, behind it. The **Öxará River**, which flows in and out of the plate towards the lake was a feature of the Viking parliament. It was recorded in the Sturlunga Saga that the river was diverted to bring fresh water within reach of the assembly. The largest island in the river, Öxarhólmar, was the site of many duels, one of the less diplomatic ways of settling a dispute. Known for their misogynist tendencies, the Vikings didn't tolerate any badly behaved women, and adulteresses and female criminals were drowned in a sack filled with heavy stones at the bridge by the church. The water is very cold and it was apparently a quick death.

Soon after Iceland adopted Christianity, around AD 1000, the King of Norway sent timber and a bell for the construction of a church at Þingvellir and it has been at the same site ever since, although the current church was rebuilt in 1907. It's beautiful inside with a font that was designed by a local farmer in 1962, and the graveyard contains the graves of two Icelandic poets and some priests of the district. The other building here, Þingvallabær, is a traditional farmhouse built in 1930 for the Alþing millennium celebrations, and now the summer residence of the president of Iceland.

Lake Þingvallavatn is a place where Europe and America come together in terms of wildlife. There are enormous amount of birds here, from the North American great northern diver and Barrow's goldeneye to the European white-tailed eagle, and given that the lake is 83 sq km in surface area and 114 m at its deepest point, with some very big fish, it's not surprising. Four species of arctic char live in the lake as well as brown trout that reputedly weigh up to 30 lb. Their average weight is around 11 lb, so the thirty-pounders may be just one of those fisherman's tales. You can fish the lake with a permit from the tourist office.

! The archaeological discovery of whale bones over 10,000 years old in the cliffs beside Hvalfjörður near Reykjavík and in Aðaldalur Valley, 3 km from the sea, has been used to plot the past shape and geography of Iceland. They indicate that sea levels were once much higher that they are now.

Best

Views to thrill

- The tectonic rift at Þingvellir, p84
- Snæfellsjökull from a boat off Stykkisholmur harbour, p93
- Puffins on the cliffs of Heimaey, p99
- The midnight sun from Grímsey, p109
- Whales breaching in the North Atlantic off Húsavík, p111

There are numerous **hiking** and **pony trekking** trails throughout Þingvellir. Many trails lead from the Þingvallabær area towards the central Skógarkot area, about 2 km away, and then either back to the tourist office or on towards the Eurasian plate at the Hrafnagjárendi rift. Tourist information centres have maps of the area with marked hiking trails and also sell permits for the two campsites (see p128). From 20th May to the end of September park rangers run free guided walking tours of Þingvellir describing the history and nature of the park. They go twice a day, at 1000 and 1400 from the church at Þingvellir and take an hour. *Íslenskir Ferðahestar* in Mosfellsbær offers riding tours of the area including midnight sun tours, see p195 for further details.

★ **Geysir**
The site is free to visit. Visitor Centre, T 480 6800, www.geysircenter.is. Summer daily 1000-1900, winter 1200-1600. ISK 450, ISK 200 children. Austurleð-SBS buses, www.austurleid.is, run year round from the BSÍ bus station to Gullfoss and Geysir, twice daily Jun-Aug, less frequently outside peak season. You can get on and off at any point; the whole circuit from Reykjavík is ISK 4400. If driving, from Þingvellir, take Route 36 until you reach Route 35 near the crater at Kerið. Continue until you pass Reykholt and then reach Geysir. From Reykjavík it's quicker to take Routes 1 and 37 south to Hveragerði then turn-off onto Route 35 just before Selfoss. Map 6, D3, p256

Letting off steam

A geyser is a hot spring formed when geothermal water gets trapped in underground fissures. The temperature of the volcanic rock (around 200 °C) heats the water but the internal pressure prevents the water from boiling at 100 °C. Boiling occurs at a much higher temperature, forming a bubble of gases that expands, forcing the water and steam up and out. The eruption lowers the pressure in the hot spring and the cycle starts again.

Because of its extreme temperature, the water dissolves substances in the surrounding rock and has a much higher concentration of minerals than other areas. In low temperature geothermal areas (less than 100 °C), the concentrations of minerals are lower and hot water can be used to directly supply water utilities. Natural steam is also harnessed to drive turbines and generate geothermal power, as well as heating for homes.

The air is heavy with sulphur, the ground smokes and water streaks high into the air. If it wasn't for all the tourists it would feel like you were on another planet. Geysir is the site of two geysers which spout regularly to the delight of onlookers. By timing your trip early or late in the day you might be able to reclaim the landscape from the coach tours and have it all to yourself.

Icelanders are proud of the fact that Geysir gave its name to all other such hot springs across the world, but today it's a lot less active than it used to be, spouting perhaps four times a day and not as high as the 70-80 m that it used to reach. Strokkur by contrast is so

! While the words and names for mountains and geysers are masculine in Icelandic, volcanoes are feminine. Apparently it's because Icelandic women are hot-tempered, unpredictable and potentially very dangerous.

regular you could set your watch by it. Water is forced 25-35 m up into the air by the build-up of steam and the resulting high pressure beneath it every three to five minutes. Make sure you've worked out which way the wind's blowing or you'll get drenched. The active hot springs were noted as far back as 1294 in the sagas and continue to be an impressive sight. Watch the pool of water and as it becomes domed you can tell it's about to blow. On a safety note, the path is clearly marked and you should take care to stick to it. The earth's crust here is very thin in places and small earthquakes can weaken the ground without showing it. Many of the pools of water here are above boiling point so care is needed.

Across the road you'll find a visitor centre, café, stables, campsite and hotel, all under the same management. This is all part of an exhibition centre showing how the forces of nature have shaped Iceland into the country it is today, with its waterfalls, volcanoes and glaciers. There's also a small folk museum tacked on to the end.

● *The Haukadalur Forest above the geysers is a well-kept secret and a great place to go riding, with wild flowers, waterfalls and fabulous views, and barely another person in sight. It costs from ISK 2000 for one hour, June to August only. Contact the Visitor Centre for contact details.*

★ Gullfoss

Easily reached and clearly marked, take Route 35 from Geysir and you'll reach Gullfoss in about 10 km. Gullfoss is a massive 2-step waterfall on the glacial River Hvítá. Map 6, D4, p256

It's a breathtaking expanse of water, beautiful at any time of year and very wet because of the spray no matter what the weather's like. In the early 1900s, Gullfoss was sold to foreign investors who wanted to harness its lucrative hydroelectric power. The local farmer's daughter, Sigríður, was opposed to the scheme and walked 110 km from the farm to Reykjavík several times to protest and enlist lawyers to stop the sale. In 1928 she won the case and at the top of the waterfall there's a monument erected to her memory.

The original geyser
This geyser is a true original and gave it's name to every other such natural feature the world over.

Snæfellsnes Peninsula

On a clear day you can see the snow-dusted heights of Snæfellsnes across the Faxaflói Bay. It's about 200 km away from the city and can be reached in a day. The peninsula has a number of small fishing villages, the largest being Stykkishólmur, with a few B&Bs. Snæfellsjökull Glacier itself has a number of claims to fame and snakes down to some strange and beautiful beaches.

▸▸ *See Sleeping p129, Tours p32*

From Reykjavík take Route 54 north of Borgarnes, Route 56 by Végamot over Kerlingarskarð and then Route 58 to Stykkishólmur. There are daily buses here from Reykjavík, ISK 3000 single, taking 3½ hrs. Seatours, (see p28) runs the car ferry Baldur across to Brjánslækur in the Western Fjords, which is the quickest way of getting there. It goes twice a day Jun-Aug, once a day Sep-May and costs ISK 1820 one way.

 Sights

Stykkishólmur
Map 6, C2, p256

The small fishing town of Stykkishólmur looks out across Breiðafjörður fjord, a haven for birdlife, seals and the occasional whale. It's the biggest town on the Snæfellsnes Peninsula but the inhabitants are well outnumbered by the wildlife. During the summer months you'll almost certainly see puffins, kittiwakes, guillemots, fulmars and the odd seal around the basalt islands offshore. It's actually impossible to count the number of small islands and skerries in the fjord as the number fluctuates according to the tide. Some of the islands were previously inhabited but nowadays the buildings that remain are only used as summer-houses, if at all. The town itself is affluent with yet another unusual church (as if there are any ordinary churches in this country), a campsite and a handful of guesthouses. From Stykkishólmur, Seatours run boat tours (see p32) into Breiðafjörður fjord including a birdwatching tour and a trip to Flatey Island where most of the buildings date from the 19th century.

Driving from Stykkishólmur towards Snæfellsjökull on Route 54 there are many scenic views. Just after the small fishing village of Grundarfjörður, have a look up at the mountain before you, Kirkjufell, shaped like a church bell and with a huge colony of seabirds living on its steep slopes. Sheep climb up here to graze but it's so steep that it's often impossible to round them up and they have to be shot down. At the foot of the mountain the sand of the beach is grey-white instead of the usual volcanic black, due to the many scallops harvested in the area.

★ Snæfellsjökull Glacier
Map 6, C1, p256

This cone-shaped glacier surrounded by a dramatic lavascape was an active volcanic area which last saw eruptions around AD 300 and has recently been turned into a national park. It occupies a special place in Icelandic iconography for a number of reasons. There's a certain literary heritage as Jules Verne chose it as the location for the start of his *Journey to the Centre of the Earth*, beginning at the small town of Arnarstapi on the south of the peninsula. Nobel prize winning novelist Halldór Laxness also took much of his inspiration from this place, which he described as a meeting of heaven and earth. It's said to be the most powerful energy point in the world, if you believe in new age theories, with a remarkable magical and healing power. And it's also the place where the world's media gathered in the 1990s to witness the first alien landing. It didn't happen, but the hoax was very convincing.

River deep, mountain high
*The rhyolite mountains of Landmannalaugar are one of Iceland's
most outstanding sights and an area of recent volcanic activity.*

Djúpalónssandur, a beach at the foot of the glacier on Route 574, captures some of the landscape's harsh beauty. There's a small 5-m-deep lagoon to your right as you walk down onto the pebbly beach and a reconstructed turf house which uses driftwood in its structure. Just before you reach it there are four large stones by the side of the track. They are of different sizes and are remembered in folktales for their use in classic tests of strength. The heaviest is 154 kg and the lightest 23 kg and they are unwieldly in shape. When you reach the beach, look out for pieces of twisted and rusted metal. They are all that remains of boats that have drifted up onto this treacherous shore in bad weather. As recently as the winter of 2001 a ship was rent asunder on these rocks, prompting a hazardous rescue mission. For this reason the beach is alternatively known as the 'ships' graveyard'. Snowmobiling and glacier trips can be taken from the town of Arnarstapi on the southern edge of Snæfellsjökull and other tours from Reykjavík also run to Snæfellsjökull, see p32.

★ Landmannalaugar

Landmannalaugar (pronounced Lant-manna-lawyer) in the central highlands is one of Iceland's beauty spots. It's an area of recent volcanic activity with huge rhyolite mountains stained sulphurous yellow and sandstone orange backing onto fields of shining obsidian chunks and rugged lava. You can relax naked in the hot mountain stream and pool in the midst of these beautiful surroundings or hike through dramatic landscapes on the four-day Laugavegurinn to the forest of Þorsmörk trek. If you want to stay longer, there's a hut at Landmannalaugar and you can camp but be aware that there are no shops in the area at all. All the main tour companies run tours here via the odd volcano or natural wonder on the way. You can combine it with a visit to Hekla, a fierce volcano that used to be known as the 'mouth of hell'.

▸▸ *See Sleeping p130, Tours p29*

Best

★ **Natural phenomena**

- Geysir, p87
- Snæfellsjökull Glacier, p93
- Volcanoes on Heimaey, p99
- The Northern Lights, p102
- Natural hot springs near Lake Mývatn, p106

The easiest way to reach the area is to drive, but make sure your car is up to it. Ideally you need a Land Rover as you may have to cross a few rivers on the way. A bus runs from the BSÍ bus station once daily at 0830 costing ISK 3760 each way – convenient for the Laugavegurinn (see below) or a brief day trip of 1¾ hrs.

 Sights

Pool
Open 24 hrs all year round. Free. Map 6, E4, p256

The pool at Landmannalaugar is great for wallowing in at any time of year – in fact, it's even better in winter if you can get there over the less reliable roads. Two streams flow into the pool, one so hot that you can't sit at its mouth and one that cools it down. Whether or not to wear swimsuits is up to you – the locals don't but most of the tourists do. Just behind the pool there's a grassy mound. Look a little closer and you'll see that it's actually a steam room with turf walls and a lava stone interior. Unfortunately earthquakes in the area have moved the heat away so now it's not very hot, but it's worth a look.

● *The benefit of taking your own transport is that you won't have to share your pool with a coachload of visitors.*

Puffin watching

The best time to watch puffins is between June and early August each year. Puffins are hunted in the Westman Islands, particularly around the clifftops above the harbour, by men wielding what looks like butterfly nets with which they swoop them down out of the sky. If you look closely you can see a small white hut perched precariously amid the cliffs above the harbour where the hunters stay during the season. Most of the cliffs here have an immense amount of birdlife and puffins also frequent the cliffs around Dalfjall and Herjólfsdalur where you can get quite close. Stórhöfði is the best place on the island to see them. You'll see a few ropes hanging from the cliffs around here too. That's where the local children monkey about on a sport called 'rappelling', basically rope-swinging, which evolved from a successful method of collecting the eggs of seabirds.

Laugavegurinn (Laugavegur Hiking Trail)
www.landmannalaugar.info *See also Tours, p32*

Also here also is Laugavegurinn, the most famous of Iceland's hikes, a four-day walk linking Landmannalaugar and the forest of Þorsmörk to the south. From Landmannalaugar to Þorsmörk the landscape drops 600 m and you have some fantastic views of the glaciers in the area, Mýrðalsjökull, Eyjafjallajökull and Tindfjallajökull, as well as the rhyolite mountains, gorges and geothermal springs. You also have the nerve-testing challenge of a few mountain rivers to cross. It's a route that can easily be done independently, but you can also have it all arranged for you by one of the tour companies.

● *A very useful pocket-sized book* The Laugavegur Hiking Trail, *by Leifur Þorsteinsson and Guðjón Magnússon, provides practical information on distances and equipment, as well as some basic maps and brief descriptions of the surroundings.*

★ Vestmannaeyjar (Westman Islands)

Puffin catchers, killer whales and killer views. Islands emerging from the sea. Volcanoes waking you up in the middle of the night. Cod fishermen millionaires. The Westman Islands are something of an attraction no matter what you're looking for and, as a local advertising slogan says, "ten million puffins can't be wrong". The archipelago of 15 islands and 30 smaller skerries just off the south coast of Iceland was created by submarine volcanic eruptions along a fissure lying southwest to northeast. This fissure threw up something special in 1963, the island of Surtsey, now a youthful 40 years old, uninhabited and closely watched by scientists as an example of how ecosystems develop. The only inhabited island of the group is Heimaey, which covers an area of just over 13 sq km with steep cliffs and two volcanoes. Locally Heimaey is better known for its wild annual festival in August when up to 10,000 people descend on the island to party, recovering the next day to catch baby puffins and send them out to sea until they get bigger. There are a number of places to go hiking in Heimaey but fortunately also enough places to hole up in if it's raining. The website www.eyjar.is/eyjar is useful.

▶▶ *See Sleeping p130, Festivals and events p181, Tours p29, Tourist Information p35*

To reach Heimaey fly or take the ferry. The Herjólfur ferry (see p31) runs twice daily from Þorlákshöfn, 1 hr by bus from Reykjavík BSÍ bus station (ISK 850). It takes 3 hrs to reach Heimaey, ISK 3600 return, ISK 1800 single. The ferry runs more frequently at the beginning of Aug for the festival, but is often fully booked at this time. Westman Islands Airline has flights from the south coast town of Bakki, taking 5 mins and costing ISK 3000-3600 for a return trip; flights from Reykjavík cost ISK 3785-6900 each way and take about 25 mins (see p25).

The Westman Islands take their name from way back in Icelandic history. The half-brother of Ingólfur Arnarson, the first settler of the country, was found slain by his Irish slaves on the south coast of

Professor Puffin

Tiny penguin-like birds with brightly coloured parrot beaks, puffins (*lundi*) are Iceland's most common birds, with over eight million pairs. It's hard to think of a more fitting national bird. The eccentric looking seabirds live in burrows like rabbits and can dive to 60 ft underwater to catch their diet of sand eels. They're nicknamed *prófastur* – 'professors' – for their clumsy gait and dinner-jacketed look.

Iceland. The slaves escaped to these islands but, in true Viking style, Ingólfur avenged the murder and brought back the women and children that they had kidnapped. The Irish were known as the Westmen, hence the Westman Islands.

The island of Heimaey has something of a tumultuous history. In 1672 Algerian pirates raided the island, killing 36 inhabitants and taking 242 into slavery. It seems a strange place to visit from Algeria and it left a huge psychological scar on the people of the island. More recently, in 1973, the people of the Westman Islands were woken up rudely in the middle of the night by a volcanic eruption. Luckily the weather had been bad and the fishing ships were in the harbour, allowing everyone to be transported to the mainland without any loss of life. The eruption continued for five months and increased the size of the island as well as burying much of the town under ash and lava. For years after the eruption the locals were able to use the heat from the cooling lava to heat their houses.

Most of the present population lived through the eruption and the result is that the small community is very close-knit, even by

! Irish monks lived in Iceland prior to the arrival of the Vikings. They thought that the devil had found some new way to defeat them in their boats by throwing burning rocks at them – what we know today as a submarine volcanic eruption.

★ **Places for birdwatching**

Best

- Grótta Beach on the Seltjarnes Peninsula, p58
- Þingvallavatn, p85
- Stykkishólmur, p92
- Vestmannaeyjar (the Westman Islands), p100
- Lake Mývatn, p106

Icelandic standards. They are some of the friendliest people in Iceland, welcoming, genuine and entertaining. The town of Heimaey is small with a couple of bakeries, a supermarket and a handful of restaurants. As this is a fishing and puffin-catching town you can expect a taste of the local specialities at reasonable prices.

◉ Sights

Eldfell and Helgafell volcanoes

The tourist information centre has a number of free maps with walking trails marked on them. The walk up Eldfell, 'fire mountain', takes about 30 mins. Map 6, F3, p256

Both of these volcanoes stand at 226 m high and are within easy walking distance of the town centre. You really need walking boots as the trail over lava is a little craggy at times. From the top of Eldfell you can see how the crater imploded on itself. Some parts of the ground are still slightly warm.

Natural history museum and aquarium

Heiðarvegur, 900 Vestmannaeyjar, **T** 481 1997. *15 May-15 Sep daily 1100-1700. ISK 300, ISK 100 children 6-13 years. Combined admission with the Folk museum ISK 450, ISK 150 children.*

Around Reykjavík

101

What are the Northern Lights?

Iceland is in the middle of the auroral zone where the northern lights, bands of colour that sweep across the sky, are most frequently seen. If the sky is dark enough and the night is clear, you should be able to see them every night. They are caused by electrically charged particles emitted by the sun reacting with the earth's magnetic field. Some electrons are drawn towards the earth, centering on the north and south poles. These reactions happen at great speed and cause the air to glow in beautiful green and pink colours.

The best places to see the northern lights are a little out of the city, although they can still be seen in a brightly lit street. About 10 km from Reykjavík, Heiðmörk is a good place that is far away from artificial light pollution, as is Nesjavallavegur, 20 km away. The best time to see them is between 2100-2400 and because of the midnight sun in summer, the best seasons are spring and autumn.

This museum houses a good range of Iceland's stones and fish, including huge cod and ugly catfish and a brilliant camera link-up to the cliff overlooking the bay so you can see the puffins wander about up close. Out the back of the museum the curator has a small puffin hospital where he helps oil-stricken and injured birds recuperate.

Folk museum and library
Raðhússtræti, 900 Vestmannaeyjar, **T** 481 1194, byggdasafn@ vestmannaeyjar.is. *Daily 1100-1700, ISK 300, ISK 100 children 6-13 years. Combined admission with the aquarium ISK 450, ISK 150 children.*

The museum is a mixture of a photographic gallery documenting the volcano eruption of 1973 and a glimpse into the past before Heimaey made its millions from fishing. There's some fishing memorabilia and remnants of life in the 19th century here too.

Westman Islands Volcano Film Show
Heiðarvegur, **T** 481 3366. *Twice daily, 3 times daily in summer. ISK 600.*

An hour-long film in English documenting the birth of Surtsey, the 1973 eruption, whale watching and island life. Worth a visit if it's raining.

Akureyri and around

Akureyri is worth visiting if only to understand why Icelanders find Reykjavík so hectic. It's the country's second-largest city, although small town is a more appropriate description, on the edge of a deep fjord surrounded by mountains. The fresh air and mountains lend the town a relaxing alpine quality. Only 40 minutes on a plane from Reykjavík, Akureyri is almost a full day's drive from the city and if you're in Iceland for a week and don't make it this far you'll miss a treat. This is what the majority of the country is like – isolated and surrounded by unrestricted natural and geological wonders.

Nearby, Lake Mývatn is home to some weird and wonderful lava formations, some bathing caves and a huge bird population, and further afield is Húsavík, recently named the best place in the world for whale watching. From here you can also reach the arctic circle – and get a certificate to prove it – on the island of Grímsey. Half of the island sits at 66° north, the only part of the country that's truly arctic. The region is great for walkers, nature lovers and birdwatchers: if you want a break from city life, this city is the place to come. The old town of Akureyri extends from the tourist information centre towards the airport. It's a random collection of corrugated-iron housing, some dating back to when the Danish settled the town, and makes for a pleasant walk despite being mainly residential. The website www.akureyri.is is a useful source of information.

▶▶ *See also Sleeping p132, Getting around p25, Tours p29*

Air Iceland, see p25, flies between Reykjavík and Akureyri twice daily in summer, once in winter (40 mins, ISK 9775 return). The airport is 2 km south of the town and buses and taxis run to and from the town centre. Coaches run once a day each way along a beautiful scenic route past the western fjords. It takes 8 hrs and costs ISK 7400 one way. In Jun-Sep it's possible to get a package where you fly one way and drive the other for around ISK 12,850. The coach station is in the centre of town next to the harbour. By car, follow Route 1 under Hvalfjörður, a toll road, and further north until your reach Akureyri. It takes around 8 hrs but there's little scope to get lost. Akureyri is 389 km from Reykjavík on the ring road. Akureyri is compact enough to explore on foot although to get to neighbouring towns and for hiking a car is invaluable. Local buses run frequently enough to let you take a day trip to other towns; during the winter it's a bit more difficult.

Sights

Akureyri Botanical Gardens
Eyrarlandsvegur, 600 Akureyri, **T** 462 7487. *1 Jun-30 Sep Fri 0800-2200, Sat-Sun 0900-2200. Map 5, D4, p255*

The gardens were opened by a group of ladies in 1912 and are the world's northernmost botanical gardens. The public gardens have botanical specimens from Iceland as well as imported flowers, trees and shrubs. The hills and dales around Akureyri, Mývatn and Húsavík contain some of the oldest forests remaining in Iceland, although many of them don't reach over 2 m high all the same. The gardens are very peaceful and worth visiting in good weather.

Kjarnaskógur Wood Recreation Area
T 462 4047.

This recreation area just inside the town towards the airport has hiking trails, woodland, playgrounds, picnic areas and some beautiful scenery and views of Eyjafjörður. Walking alongside the streams and larch trees is fun on a good day if you don't have the energy to make it as far as Mývatn. You can still see the remains of old peasant farms amid the trees too.

Akureyri Art Museum

Kaupvangsstræti 12, 600 Akureyri, **T** 461 2610, www.artak.strik.is.
Tue-Sun 1300-1800. ISK 400. Map 5, C4, p255

One of the youngest art museums in Iceland, Akureyri Art Museum displays modern Icelandic art, especially local art, and a variety of international touring exhibitions including collaborations with Lapland and Greenland. Kaupvangsstræti is known as the art canyon as it's the centre of the artistic movement in Akureyri.

Akureyri Museum

Aðalstræti 58, 602 Akureyri, **T** 462 4162, www.akmus.is.
1 Jun-15 Sep daily 1000-1700, 16 Sep-31 May Sat 1400-1600 and by arrangement. ISK 400; joint ticket with Nonni's House ISK 500.
Map 5, G5, p255

A small historical museum in the old town tracing the settlement of the Eyjafjörður district and the town of Akureyri itself. It displays anything from family life, fishing and settlement, heathen burial customs and historic photography, all of which looks back to a simpler and harder way of living.

Nonni's House (Nonnahús)

Aðalstræti 54, 600 Akureyri, **T** 462 3555, www.nonni.is. *1 Jun-31 Aug daily 1 000-1700, otherwise by arrangement. ISK 300; joint ticket with Akureyri Museum ISK 500. Map 5, G5, p255*

This wooden building next to the Akureyri Museum is the childhood home of the children's author Nonni, the Reverend Jón Sveinsson, dating from the mid-1800s. He's primarily known in Germany and France for his children's stories.

The Christmas Garden (Jólagarðurinn)

Eyjafjarðarsveit, 601 Akureyri, **T** 463 1433. *Jun-Aug 1000-2200, Sep-Dec 1400-2200, Christmas 1400-1800, Jan-May 1400-1800.*

If you've always wanted to know how the Icelandic tradition about the 13 yuletide lads started or want to know more about other Icelandic folk traditions surrounding Christmas, this is the place to come. This small café/shop/museum specializing in all things Yuletide is past the airport south of Akureyri. The café serves traditional food too, including cakes and *hangikjöt* (smoked lamb).

Lake Mývatn

The tourist information centre in Akureyri has information about Lake Mývatn and the surrounding area and there's a commercial tourist centre at Reykjahlíð, Eldá Tourist Centre where you can buy fishing permits, hire bikes, arrange accommodation and buy postcards. Buses run twice daily to Reykjahlíð from Akureyri bus station and guided coach tours of the area go once daily. Map 6, B6, p256

Mývatn is the top tourist destination in the area, a beautiful lake broken up with unusual lava formations. The name means 'midge lake' and there are two types of midge that live here, one that likes humans and one that doesn't. They are both essential to the eco- system around here as there are lots of fish in the water and a massive bird population, including the North American Barrow's Goldeneye. The main drop-off point for buses is the village of Reykjahlíð where there is a café, hotel, campsite and sourvenir shops.

To have longer periods of twilight, when colour is not bleached but extremely rich, one has to go North. In June the sun never sets at all. You can see the landscape at all hours, 24 hours a day. I found myself deeply attracted to it, and I went to Iceland twice to tour the island. You get a beautiful light with long shadows. There's no one there. I'd use a little sketchbook. A bit later, I'd do a watercolour back in the hotel.

David Hockney, The Times, 16 December, 2002.

The route to Mývatn from Akureyri takes you past **Góðafoss**, an 11-m-high waterfall whose name means the 'waterfall of the pagan gods'. At the Alþing in AD 1000, Þorgeir, the district commissioner of this area, was the decision maker for whether Iceland should embrace the new Christianity rather than stay faithful to their old pagan gods. He decided that since the Christian god was kind, just and benevolent it would be a better choice than the impetuous and often cruel Norse gods and so Iceland was Christianized. On his return from Þingvellir to the north, he cast his statues of pagan gods into this waterfall.

Around Mývatn itself there are a number of things to see that you can't see anywhere else in the world as a result of the way it has been formed by volcanic activity. The lake itself is 37 sq km but doesn't look that big because it is peppered with islands and birds. Mývatn lies on the boundary of the Eurasian and North American plates and the volcanic activity in the area is ongoing. There is only one real town here, Reykjahlíð, where there are a couple of hotels, a campsite and a café-restaurant. Within walking distance of the town you'll find **Grjótagjá**. This was once a popular bathing spot with two caves, one the right temperature and one a little too cold. Volcanic activity in the area has shifted the hot spot so that now the warmer cave is too warm at 60°C but the cold one is just right.

Along the eastern side of the lake you'll find the weird lava formations of the **Dimmuborgir**. These rambling cliffs and scarred pillars of lava are known as the 'dark castles' in Icelandic and you can see why. A pool of molten lava was formed here after an eruption that drained away towards Mývatn and left columns standing behind it, twisted and etched with horizontal lines. Some similar lava shapes were found at the bottom of the sea off the coast of Mexico, but none exist anywhere else on dry land.

There are a huge number of **walks** to take in the area, mainly clearly marked. Further details can be found in the tourist office at Akureyri where they have a booklet on the area containing walking routes. Hitch-hiking is common and safe.

Lake Myvatn Nature Baths

Jardbadshólar, 660 Mývatn, **T** 464 4411, www.jardbodin.is.
Summer daily 0900-2400; winter Mon-Fri 1600-2200, Sat-Sun
1200-2200. ISK 1100, ISK 550 8-16 year olds, under 7s free.

Set in the mountains near Namaskard, this is a less crowded and
less commercial version of the Blue Lagoon, and the naturally
heated pool and steam bath offer a relaxing way to spend a
morning or afternoon. The lagoon itself is man-made and the
water temperature averages 36-40°C. The high concentration of
minerals, silicates and geothermal microorganisms is reputed
to be particularly beneficial for your skin.

The islands of Eyjafjörður

The peaceful islands of Grímsey and Hrísey are like teardrops in the
middle of Eyafjörður. Grímsey is the more popular of the two. In fact,
it's a slight cliché to Icelanders that all tourists come to their country to
take a trip to the Golden Circle and visit Grímsey. In reality, visiting this
small island isn't as easy as it seems, but what other chance will you
have to visit the Arctic Circle in a day? Day trips or overnight stays can
be arranged for both islands.

▸▸ *See Sleeping p136, Tours p29, Map 6, A5, p256*

 Sights

Grímsey

It takes 3 hrs to reach the island by boat (Jun-Aug Mon, Wed and Fri,
twice weekly in winter). A bus from Akureyri, leaving at 0730, is the
easiest way to get there. The bus connects with the Sæfari ferry at Dalvík
(see p28). For a day trip, the bus also meets the incoming ferry in the
evening. A return trip including the bus is ISK 4000; ferry only ISK 3500.

▶ Whale watching

Húsavík has been named the best place to see whales in the world by the WWF. However, it isn't really worth trekking up to Húsavík for the whales on their own as you can see much the same from Reykjavík. The most common whales seen here are minke whales, with a similar percentage sighting of 95.4% and a similar price of ISK 3500-4000. There is however a slightly greater chance of seeing a humpback whale here, but the chances of seeing a blue whale or an orca are still as slim as 0.2-0.6%. The main advantage is the chance to find out about what you're seeing at the excellent Whale Watching Centre.

Grímsey is Iceland's northernmost inhabited island, the home of a fishing community of 95. It's a good place to see seabirds and probably offers the best view in the world of the midnight sun in July. Grímsey also has a church, café, swimming pool and guesthouse.

Hrísey

The Eyfar ferry (see p28) goes to Hrísey from Árskógssandur, 35 km north of Akureyri, once an hour 0900-2300 15 Jun-15 Aug, less frequently in winter. It takes 15 mins and costs ISK 350 each way. The bus trip from Akureyri to Árskógssandur costs ISK 550 each way and is also the local delivery van. It goes once daily from Akureyri bus station.

Hrísey is a tiny island with walking trails, one cow and around 270 inhabitants. It's actually the biggest island off the coast of Iceland after Heimaey in the Westman Isles and 7½ km wide at its broadest point. Well-marked walking trails take you around the south of the island but the north has restricted access to protect a colony of breeding eider duck. It's a peaceful and relaxing place to go walking with 40 species of birds, corrugated-iron-clad houses and lots of grassland. Watch out for divebombing arctic terns. As you look out towards the eastern mountains of the fjord, look up at the tallest peak, Kaldbakur. It's another of Iceland's powerful new-age energy points. You can also see clearly how the glacier gouged out the fjord. Hrísey also has a guesthouse, swimming pool, church and restaurant and is a great place for a day trip if you like birdwatching, walking and peace and quiet.

Húsavík

Húsavík, 91 km from Akureyri on the edge of the next bay along, Skjálfandi, is a small, pretty fishing town best known for its whale-watching trade. The town itself is very small with a couple of tourist shops, cafés and guesthouses and some excellent museums, including the world's only penis museum, recently relocated from Reykjavík. The website www.husavik.is is a useful source of infomation.
▸ *See Sleeping p136, Tours p33, Map 6, A6, p256*

From Akureyri, buses run to Húsavík 5 times a day from late May to the end of Aug, ISK 1800, 1 hr 10 mins. Outside this tourist season they run only twice daily. By car it's a 30-min drive away to the north.

◉ Sights

Whale Watching Centre
Hafnarstéttinni, 640 Húsavík, **T** 464 2520, www.icewhale.is. *May and Sep daily 1000-1700, 1 Jun-1 Sep daily 0900-2100, 1 Oct -30 Apr Sat-Sun 1200-1600. ISK 400, ISK 150 children.*

Lots of anecdotes about whales and whaling in Iceland and a huge array of things to look at, all housed in the old slaughter house. It's the only whaling museum in Iceland and is worth visiting if you're in the area. They also offer fish-factory tours. Very good for children and adults alike.

Iceland Phallological Museum

Hedinsbraut 3a, 640 Húsavík, **T** 566 8668, www.phallus.is.
20 May-10 Sep daily 1200-1800. ISK 500.

It's the only penis museum in the world, proudly exhibiting
members belonging to nearly all the mammals in a single country,
including a human foreskin. In addition to the biological section of
the museum, visitors can view the collection of over 150 penises and
penile parts as well as artistic oddments and other practical utensils
related to the museum´s chosen theme. There are 38 species from
15 different types of whale, all neatly organized and stored in jars,
one over 6 ft tall. Other specimens include a polar bears, seals and
walrus. The exhibit is the brainchild of a local teacher who has been
collecting since 1974. He's waiting in anticipation for a donation
from a 90-year-old Icelandic womanizer who's signed his anatomy
away when he dies!

Húsavík Folk Museum and Library

Stóragarði 17, 640 Húsavík, **T** 464 1860, www.husmus.is. *Jun-Aug
daily 1000-1800. Sep-May Mon-Fri 0900-1700, Sun 1600-1800. ISK 300
including free drinks in the café.*

Excellent museum covering all areas of life in the North from
folk tales, natural history and maritime memorabilia to district
archives and paintings. Look out for the big polar bear, shot in
1969 on Grímsey, and the weird fish like the deep-sea gulper.
Well worth visiting.

Húsavík Church

Jun-Aug 0900-1200 and 1300-1800.

Built by the first architect of Iceland, the small church in the village
is pretty and overlooks the harbour. There has been a church and
priest in the town since 1231.

Sleeping

Reykjavík has a good range of accommodation, from high-class hotels to family-run B&Bs. There's plenty of choice in the city centre, close to the action, but be prepared to pay for the convenience. Most of the hotels are stylish, modern and expensive, but there's also a wide range of good quality guesthouses, particularly in summer, and if you take your sleeping bag you can often sleep for half-price at hostels and guesthouses, which keeps the price down without sacrificing a private room or plump mattress.

As the city becomes ever more popular places fill up quickly so you need to book two to three days in advance in the summer months. Prices drop considerably in September and sleeping-bag accommodation is more readily available out of season. You can also hire studios and apartments in the city centre or stay on farms a little out of town to experience an alternative view of Icelandic life. Outside the city, prices are a little higher but there are guesthouses and sleeping-bag accommodation in all the main towns and villages.

Sleeping codes

Price

L	Above ISK 19,500
A	ISK 15,800-19,500
B	ISK 11,800-15,700
C	ISK 9,100-11,700
D	ISK 6,600-9000
E	ISK 4000-6,500
F	ISK 2,600-3,900
G	Under ISK 2,600

Prices are per night for a double room in high season

The tourist information centre can book accommodation for a small price, www.tourist.reykjavik.is. Visit www.hotel.connect.com for some good-value packages.

101 Reykjavík

Hotels

L Hotel 101, Hverfisgata 10, **T** 580 0101, www.101hotel.is. *Map 2, E5, p250* Opposite the Culture House and the National Opera, this new and ultra-fashionable boutique outfit has sculptures, murals, Icelandic art and an airy bar and restaurant. It's all very minimalist chic with lots of reflective surfaces, huge showers and freestanding baths. The spa and gym downstairs will help you keep as glam as the surroundings. If you like what you find, you can take most of it with you, from the Icelandic wool rug to the Italian linen – at a price of course. Rates drop a little from October to April.

L Hotel Borg, Pósthússtræti 11, **T** 551 1440, www.hotelborg.is
Map 2, E3, p250 Reykjavík's finest, an art-deco hotel in
Austurvöllur Square with lovingly preserved rooms and modern
art. It's a movie-star haunt where Catherine Deneuve stayed
when she came to visit Björk. *Hótel Borg* was Iceland's first luxury
hotel, built by a wrestler in the 1930s and retains great wide
shower heads for a serious dose of glamour.

L Hotel Holt, Bergstaðastræti 37, **T** 552 5700, www.holt.is *Map
2, G4, p251* On a quiet street in central Reykjavík, *Hotel Holt* is a
Relais & Châteaux boutique hotel with an elegant interior, large
Modern Art collection, expansive rooms and seafood delicacies in
the restaurant. A luxury experience.

L Hotel Plaza, Aðalstraeti 4, www.plaza.is. *Map 2, D2, p250*
Central location across the square from the tourist information
centre. 105 well appointed and recently refurbished rooms with
tasteful modern furniture.

L Hotel Reykjavík Centrum, Aðalstraeti 16, **T** 514 6000,
www.hotelcentrum.is *Map 2, D2 , p252* Elegant new hotel on
one of the city's most historic streets. During its construction the
remains of a Viking longhouse from the Settlement Period were
found and a new museum is set to open in 2006 (see p41).
Set over three buildings, the hotel has plenty of character and
combines early 1900s style with modern luxury and facilities.
Angular ceilings, plenty of glass and neutral colours create a
feeling of space and calm. The restaurant specializes in Icelandic
cuisine while the cosy bar is a good place to relax.

L Radisson SAS 1919 Hotel, Pósthússtræti 2, **T** 599 1000,
www.1919.reykjavik.radissonsas.com *Map 2, D3, p251* Classy hotel
in the historic building of a former shipping company, dating from
1919. Features include a grand marble staircase, sculptures and

> ★ **Designer/boutique hotels**
>
> Best
> - Hotel 101, p115
> - Hotel Borg, p116
> - Hotel Holt, p116
> - The Tower Guesthouse, p117
> - Hotel Klöpp, p117

Sleeping

good harbour views. Rooms are immaculate with high ceilings and flat screen TV. It offers a more personal service than most business hotels. The restaurant is run by award-winning chef and serves modern world cuisine. The funky *Salt Lounge Bar* is popular at weekends and Reykjavík's original hot dog stand is just outside (p147).

L-A Hótel Klöpp, Klapparstígur 26, **T** 511 6062, www.centerhotels.com. *Map 2, E6, p250* Fashionable central hotel with rooms and studios. Sleek modern design, neutral and beige colours and wooden floors. Klöpp means 'stone' or 'rock' and it has great views of Mount Esja. Recommended.

L-D Tower Guesthouse, Grettisgata 6, **T** 896 6694, www.tower.is. *Map 2, G8, p251* Luxurious central guesthouse and apartments with elegant rooms, kitchens and bathrooms in a refined and courtly atmosphere. Double rooms, apartments and suites available. Outstanding top-class accommodation, with a jacuzzi on a balcony overlooking the bay. Discount of 10% on rates for a week or more.

A Hotel Óðinsvé, Óðinstorg, **T** 511 6200, www.hotelodinsve.is . *Map 2, G5, p251* An elegant, well-located hotel with a good line in stuffed seabirds. The name means 'the sanctuary of Odin', the highest of the Norse gods, and the restaurant next door, *Siggi Hall*, is outstanding. Thick carpets, polished wood and a refined ambience.

117

A Hotel Skjaldbreið, Laugavegur 16, **T** 511 6060, www.centerhotels.com. *Map 2, E5, p250* Modern, comfortable hotel in one of the city's converted stately homes. Family-run, airy and stylish, in the centre of the city with large rooms. Perfect for a relaxed stay in the thick of the action.

B Fosshótel Baron, Barónsstígur 2-4, **T** 562 3204, www.fosshotel.is. *Map 2, F9, p250* Part of the Fosshótel chain. Bright, modern and functional hotel with en suite doubles and apartments, centrally located and with all mod cons.

B Hótel Frón, Laugavegi 22a, **T** 511 4666, www.hotelfron.is. *Map 2, F6, p250* *Hótel Frón* looks like it's made of blue and orange Lego bricks and contains 54 rooms as well as new modern apartments. The bright studios all have kitchenettes and are stylish and fresh. There's a restaurant and bar downstairs.

B Metropolitan Hotel, Ránargata 4a, **T** 511 1155, www.metropolitan.is. *Map 2, C1, p250* In a particularly nice part of town, newly renovated and very comfortable, the *Metropolitan* is a friendly, small hotel with a personal touch. Prices significantly cheaper in off-season.

B-C Hótel Leifur Eiríksson, Skólavörðustígur 45, **T** 562 0800, www.hotelleifur.is. *Map 2, H6, p251* In a great location next to the Halgrímskirkja church, so you can always find your way home. Good-value hotel with friendly staff, personal service and breakfast provided in the café/coffee bar. Comfortable and relaxed.

C 4th Floor Hotel, Laugavegur 101, **T** 511 3030, www.4thfloor hotel.is. *Map 2, F8, p251* In the same building as *Guesthouse 101*, below. Spacious, modern rooms with wooden floors and kitsch zebra print fabrics that you'll either love or hate. The smart breakfast room feels more like a bar. Good views out to sea.

C **Guesthouse 101**, Laugavegur 101, **T** 562 6101, www.iceland101.is. *Map 2, F8, p250* Modern and spacious guesthouse with moderate-sized rooms in the centre of the city, with a bus stop right outside. Ideal location for shopping, drinking and dining in a large concrete building just off the main street.

C **Guesthouse Adam**, Skólavörðustígur 42, **T** 896 0242, www.adam.is *Map 2, G6, p251* Small guesthouse close to Hallgrímskirkja with self-contained rooms with kitchen facilities and a grocery store next door. Very close to the main street, purpose-built accommodation where guests are left to their own devices. Free internet for guests and car hire available.

D **Álfhóll Guesthouse**, Ránargata 8, **T** 898 1838, www.islandia.is /alf *Map 2, C1, p250* The friendly 'elves' house' has five double rooms, two single rooms and a studio apartment, all well looked after and furnished in rustic style. Clean, friendly and recommended, especially if you're otherworldly. Open in summer only.

D **Anna's Guesthouse**, Smaragata 16, **T** 562 1618, anna.s@mmedia.is. *Map 2, J4, p250* Located in the former Czechoslovakian Embassy building, rooms are spacious and well decorated. Anna lived in America for 30 years, is very helpful and speaks excellent English.

D **Butterfly Guesthouse**, Ránargata 8a, **T** 894-1864, www.kvasir.is/butterfly. *Map 2, C1, p251* Cosy guesthouse on a quiet street in central Reykjavík. Fully-equipped kitchen. Singles, doubles and a two-room apartment. Open in summer only.

D **Domus Guesthouse**, Veghúsastígur 7, **T** 5611200, www.domus guesthouse.is. *Map 2, C1, p250* Formerly the Norwegian embassy, this friendly guesthouse has 12 spacious doubles and plenty of sleeping-bag accommodation. Breakfast is included.

D Guesthouse Aurora, Freyjugata 24, **T** 899 1773, www.aurorahouse.is. *Map 2, I6, p251* Neat, newly refurbished guesthouse near Hallgrímskirkja open in summer only, offers cheaper sleeping-bag accommodation at ISK 2200. Central and friendly.

D Guesthouse Centrum, Njálsgata 74, **T** 511 5600, www.guesthouse-centrum.com. *Map 2, E2, p250* Spacious guesthouse/hotel beside the town pond with bike hire and refined atmosphere. Great location, views and large, comfortable rooms, breakfast included. Recommended.

D Guesthouse Ísafold, Bárugata 11, **T** 561 2294, www.itn.is/~isafold *Map 2, C1, p250* Friendly, individual family-style lodgings offering a large breakfast and cosy rooms in an old house close to the old harbour with a shared kitchen.

D Guesthouse Víkingur, Ránargata 12, **T** 562 1290, www.simnet.is/ghviking. *Map 2, C1, p250* Only open in summer, this is a small well-kept guesthouse in a nice quiet part of town, with car rental. Compact and family friendly.

D Hólmfríður, Skólavörðustígur 16, **T** 562 5482, holmfridur@ holmfridur.is. *Map 2, G6, p251* Eight rooms in the centre of the city with great views from the fifth floor. Small family-style bed and breakfast.

D Snorri's Guesthouse, Snorrabraut 61, **T** 552 0598, www.guesthousereykjavik.com. *Map 2, J9, p250* Single, double and family rooms. Facilities include a fully-equipped kitchen, cosy dining room with a large screen TV, as well as a patio and garden. Sleeping-bag accommodation is also available.

★ **Sleeping-bag accommodation**

Best

- Domus Guesthouse, p119
- Guesthouse Aurora, p120
- Salvation Army Guest House, p121
- Hotel Floki, p124
- Guesthouse Regínu, p124

D Travel Inn Guesthouse, Sóleyjargata 31, **T** 561 3553, www.dalfoss.is *Map 2, J4, p251* Medium-sized guesthouse with a sauna, family rooms and shared bathrooms. Rooms are small but the service is good.

E Einar's B&B, Bræðraborgarstígur 43, 1st floor, **T** 698 4745, einartj@simnet.is. *Map 1, E1, p248* Einar has two rooms open in the summer for basic B&B accommodation in the quiet eastern part of town close to the old harbour and a swimming pool.

E Guesthouse Jörð, Skólavörðustígur 13a, **T** 562 1739. *Map 2, G6, p251* Recommended great-value friendly guesthouse in the centre of the city with breakfast included and a cosy atmosphere. Large airy rooms and personal service.

E Guesthouse Sunna, Þórsgata 26, **T** 511 5570, www.sunna.is. *Map 2, H6, p251* Modern family-style guesthouse in the shadow of Hallgrímskirkja with kitchen facilities and a variety of rooms.

G Salvation Army Guest House, Kirkjustræti 2, **T** 561 3203, www.guesthouse.is *Map 2, E2, p250* The cheapest accommodation in the centre, with small shared rooms and a kitchen. Bathrooms are shared and it's a bit of a squeeze. The best value sleeping-bag accommodation for the location.

Sleeping

Houses and apartments for rent

A-B Apartments, Skálholtsstígur 2a, **T** 511 2166, www.mmedia.is/apartment *Map 2, G3, p251* Just across the pond by the National Gallery, these apartments have wonderful views and are fully furnished with no minimum stay. Light, relaxed and well looked after.

B Luna Apartments, Spítalistígur 1, **T** 511 2800, www.luna.is. *Map 2, F4, p250* Bright, friendly and well-kept apartments in a beautiful 1920s house in the centre of Reykjavík. The comfortable luxury apartments are big enough for four people and there's a 10% discount for a stay of a week or more.

B-D Lighthouse Apartments, Vitastígur 11, **T** 699 6277. *Map 2, G8, p250* Just off Laugervegur, this big red house built in 1906, has six fully furnished apartments with bathroom and kitchette, and two rooms. Good discounts in winter.

C Room with a View, Laugavegur 18, **T** 896 2559, www.roomwithaview.is *Map 2, F6, p250 See also p203* Sleek modern studios and apartments above *Mál og Menning* bookshop on the main street in the heart of town, with bike hire. Perfectly located, luxurious and spacious. Panoramic city views, balconies and even jacuzzis.

D Hóll Cottage, Grjótagata 12, **T** 5512044, www.simnet.is/holl. *Map 2, D2, p250* Charming cottage built in 1895. Lovingly restored to its original condition and tastefully furnished with both antique and modern furniture.

Laugardalur Valley and city outskirts

Hotels and guesthouses

L Grand Hotel Reykjavík, Sigtún 38, 105 Reykjavík, **T** 514 8000, www.grand.is. *Map 3, D6, p252* Stylish modern business-class hotel with Icelandic restaurant and opulent interior. Large rooms, many with balconies and a view of Mount Esja. Good service and range of tours.

L Radisson SAS Saga Hotel, Hagatorg, 107 Reykjavík, **T** 525 9900, www.radissonsas.is. *Map 1, F1, p248* Immense modern Radisson hotel located just beyond the city pond and the library. Scandinavian, stylish interior with all imaginable facilities, bar, restaurant and classy professional service.

A Hótel Nordica, Hlíðarfótur, **T** 444 4500, www.icehotel.is. *Map 3, E6, p252* This huge Icelandair hotel has modern facilities and stylish chrome, glass and natural wood decor. The service is excellent but the sheer size of the place can make it feel overwhelming. Rooms at the front have excellent views over Mount Esja.

B Fosshótel Lind, Rauðarárstígur 18, 105 Reykjavík, **T** 562 3350, www.fosshotel.is *Map 3, D1, p252* Part of the luxury Fosshótel chain, with all mod cons and a business market but also open for tourists. A little out of town but not too far to walk.

B Hótel Vík, Síðumúla 19, 108 Reykjavík, **T** 588 5588, www.hotelvik.is. *Map 3, G8, p253* Small three-star hotel with restful rooms with kitchenettes located near to Kringlan mall on the edge of Reykjavík. Cosy, homely and an easy distance from Laugardalur Valley.

C Hotel Cabin, Borgartún 32, 105 Reykjavík, **T** 511 6030, www.hotelcabin.is. *Map 3, B5, p252* Medium-sized modern hotel on the edge of 101 Reykjavík next to the main road, with relaxed service and reasonable-sized rooms. *Hotel Cabin* is well situated near to the main shopping area and has good views of the bay.

C Hótel Flóki, Flókagata 1, 105 Reykjavík, **T** 552 1155, www.eyjar.is/guesthouse/english/english.htm *Map 3, E1, p252* Compact hotel/guesthouse within walking distance of the centre of Reykjavík, with shared kitchen, garden and continental breakfast included. Also offers camping, fishing and pony-trekking and cheaper sleeping-bag accommodation at ISK 2500-3000.

C Guesthouse Kríunes by Lake Elliðavatn, **T** 567 2245, www.kriunes.is. *13 km from the centre of the city.* This guesthouse has seven rooms and a campsite, sleeping-bag accommodation for six to eight people, great views, and is good for walking in the area. It's 3 km from the swimming pool. Restful and relaxing.

D Guesthouse Dúna, Suðurhlíð 35d, 105 Reykjavík, **T** 588 2100, www.islandia.is/duna. *Map 1, G7, p249* Not a pretty building, but offers a big breakfast buffet and functional rooms just off the main road and near to the Pearl. Sleeping-bag accommodation for ISK 1950 per night.

D Guesthouse Regínu, Mjölnisholt 14, 105 Reykj vík, **T** 551 2050, www.guesthouseregina.com. *Map 3, D2, p252* Basic guesthouse with 20 rooms and an apartment studio. 15-minute walk from the centre of town, cooking facilities and breakfast included. Sleeping-bag accommodation also available.

E Hótel Atlantis, Grensásvegur 14, 108 Reykjavík, **T** 588 0000, www.atlantis.is *Map 3, H9, p253* Small and friendly hotel in the suburbs of Reykjavík with very good value rooms and a warm atmosphere. Also offers car hire, free internet, breakfast and bathrobes. Studios and triple rooms available.

Houses and apartments for rent

D Elliðahvammur, by Vatnsendi. **T** 567 4656, www.hvammur.is. A six-person cottage with two rooms for a relaxing stay in the countryside. It's 5 km from the city centre in the Elliðaar Valley, not far from Árbær on Route 410, and reachable by bus.

D Pávi Guesthouse/apartments, Brautarholt 4, 105 Reykjavík, **T** 899 9981. *Map 3, D4, p252* Modern studio apartments, six two-bed apartments and eight double rooms. Clean and luxurious, internet, laundry and close to Laugavegur on the outskirts of town. Sleeping-bag accommodation also available from ISK 1600 per night.

Hostels and campsites

G City campsite, Sundlaugavegur 34, 105 Reykjavík, **T** 568 6944, www.reykjavikcampsite.is. *Map 3, B8, p253* Open 15 May to 15 September, possibly a little earlier by arrangement with the youth hostel next door. It also has cabins for hire, a decent laundry and toilet block, and bike hire.

G Reykjavík City Youth Hostel, Sundlaugavegur 34, 105 Reykjavík, **T** 553 8110, www.hostel.is. *Map 3, B8, p253* Right next to the sports and recreation centre, this is the best hostel in Iceland. Cheerful, informed staff and 170 beds in a newly built modern building. Dorms for two to six people or private rooms available. Kitchens, laundry and table tennis. It's a 40-minute walk from the centre of Reykjavík in Laugardalur, or a 10-minute bus ride.

Öskjuhlíð Hill

Hotels and guesthouses

A Hótel Lóftleiður, Hlíðarfótur, **T** 444 4500, www.icehotel.is.
Map 1, G4, p248 Classy, modern hotel with a restaurant,
swimming pool and refined Scandinavian-style interior despite
the ugly building. First-class treatment from the city's top hotel
chain where visiting dignitaries often stay.

Hafnarfjörður

Hotels and guesthouses

C-D Viking Hotel, Strandgata 56, 220 Hafnarfjörður, **T** 565 1213,
www.vikinghotel.biz. *Map 4, F3, p254* Luxury accommodation in
the Viking village with 29 rooms all decorated in accordance with
Icelandic, Faroese and Greenlandic style.

D Guesthouse Berg, Bæjarhraun 4, 220 Hafnarfjörður,
T 565 2220, lobby@gestberg.is. *Map 4, B6, p254* Large modern
guesthouse with 25 rooms, some sleeping six, and activities
from golfing to horse riding and whale watching can be
arranged. Breakfast included.

D The Guesthouse by the Lake, Lækjarkinn 2, 220
Hafnarfjörður, **T** 565 5132, http://frontpage.simnet.is/olgunn.
Map 4, F6, p254 Small and friendly family-run accommodation
with breakfast buffet and self-catering facilities. Four rooms and
shared bathrooms.

D Studio Apartment, Hraunbrún 25, 220 Hafnarfjörður, **T** 555 2712, jonsonb@mi.is. *Map 4, C4, p254* Spacious, clean studio flat accommodating two to four people. Exciting modern architecture.

D Helguhús, Lækjarkinn 8, 220 Hafnarfjörður; **T** 555 2842, www.helguhus.is. *Map 4, F6, p254* Cosy private lodgings with a genial host and rooms sleeping up to three people. The studio apartment for up to six people costs ISK 12,250 per night. Close to the swimming pool.

Hostels and campsites

G Hafnarfjörður Guesthouse and campsite, Hjallabraut 51, 220 Hafnarfjörður, **T** 565 0900, www.hafnarfjordurguesthouse.is. *Map 4, B2, p254* Summer only. Affordable guesthouse next to Víðistaðatún sculpture garden, 1½ km from the centre. Comfortable dorms and private rooms. Helpful staff can help with tour bookings. Facilities include kitchen, washing machines, lounge and internet.

Blue Lagoon

Hotels

A Northern Light Inn, Blue Lagoon Rd, 240 Grindavik, **T** 426 8650, www.nli.is. *Map 6, E2, p256* *Courtesy transfer from Keflavík Airport provided, 40 mins from Reykjavík on Route 41 and 43, the Blue Lagoon bus leaves the BSÍ coach station in Reykjavík 4 times daily.* This is the only hotel near the Blue Lagoon. 20 quiet and spacious rooms with geothermal showers and Icelandic down duvets. Discounts available for more two night stays or longer. A good spot for relaxing in a fluffy bathrobe and pampering yourself.

Golden Circle

Hotels and guesthouses

C Hótel Brattholt, Gulfoss, **T** 486 8991, brattholtii@islandia.is.
7 km from Geysir and 3 km from Gulfoss. Map 6, D4, p256 Brattholt
is a small country hotel offering traditional Icelandic food and small
and basic rooms. Friendly service and a great view, this is a good
hotel for walkers.

B-F Hotel Geysir, Haukadal, 801 Selfoss, **T** 486 8915,
www.geysircenter.is. *Map 6, D3, p256* Wooden alpine-style hotel
in the middle of nowhere with fine views of the geysers and an
outdoor thermal pool as well as horse riding. Unusual and good
value with cabins, apartments, double rooms and dormitory
accommodation. Breakfast buffet from ISK 1050.

Hostels and campsites

G There are two camping areas in Þingvellir – *Leirar* is adjacent
to the tourist centre (see p84) and the road, while *Vatnskot* is
situated at an abandoned farmhouse beside Þingvallavatn lake at
Vatnskot. They are both fairly basic with toilet facilities and you
need to buy a permit at the tourist information centre on arrival.
It costs ISK 500 per night for adults, under 16s are free and senior
citizens pay ISK 250. See www.thingvellir.is/english/
national-park/camping for details.

Snæfellsnes Peninsula

Hotels and guesthouses

B-C Hotel Stykkishólmur, Borgarbraut 8, **T** 430 2100,
hotelstykkishomur@simnet.is. *Map 6, C2, p256* Modern hotel
with fantastic views from its hill-top location. Smart dining area
but bedrooms are on the small side. Discounts in available in the
low season.

D Heimagisting Maríu, Höfðagata 11, 340 Stykkishólmur,
 T 438 1258. *Map 6, C2, p256* Cosy private accommodation with
a friendly host in the centre of Stykkishólmur with a shared kitchen
and attic rooms. Simple but welcoming.

G Stykkishólmur Youth Hostel, Höfðagata 1, 340
Stykkishólmur, **T** 438 1095, www.hostel.is *Map 6, C2, p256* Great
views from this popular corrugated-iron-clad hostel, one of the
town's oldest buildings. Also runs boat and bird-watching tours
and you'll need to book in advance in the summer.

Hostels and campsites

G Campsite, off Aðalgata, Stykkishólmur, **T** 438 1150. The
campsite is near the swimming pool and golf course. Basic
facilities include toilets and sinks. ISK 500 per person.

Sleeping

Landmannalaugar

Hostels and campsites

G Skáli Fí, **T** 568 2533, www.fi.is *Map 6, E4, p256* Run by the Icelandic Hiking Association. Basic wooden hut with 75 beds and a campsite, kitchen and impressive modern steel bathroom facilities. Offers horse riding and a perfect location beside the natural hot pool. Open all year round but book as far in advance as possible. Camping is available for ISK 600.

Vestmannaeyjar (Westman Islands)

Hotels and guesthouses

B Hótel Þórshamar, Vestmannabraut 28, 900 Vestmannaeyjar, **T** 481 2900, http://hotel.eyjar.is. Classy business-style hotel in the middle of Heimaey with all mod cons and certainly the best that the Westman Islands have to offer. There's a jacuzzi, sauna and snooker room in the basement.

D Guesthouse Hamar, Herjólfsgata 4, 900 Vestmannaeyjar, **T** 481 3400, http://hotel.eyjar.is. Smart guesthouse owned by *Hótel Þórshamar* in the centre of town with comfortable rooms. Sleeping-bag accommodation also available from ISK 4500.

D-E Hotel Eyjar, Bárustígur 2, on the corner of Starndvegur, 900 Vestmannaeyjum, **T** 481-3636, www.hoteleyjar.eyjar.is. Large, comfortable hotel. Rooms are more like apartments with bathrooms and kitchens. Good value.

E Guesthouse Hreiðrið, Faxastígur 33, 900 Vestmannaeyjar, **T** 481 1045. Sleeping-bag accommodation from ISK 1700, kitchen facilities and private rooms available in this small, central guesthouse.

E Guesthouse María, Brekastígur 37, 900 Vestmannaeyjar, **T** 481 2744. Well-kept guesthouse with eight bedrooms, cooking facilities and breakfast. Clean and friendly. Sleeping-bag accommodation for ISK 2500.

E Guesthouse Sunnuhól, Vestmannabraut 28, 900 Vestmannaeyjar, **T** 481 2900, http://hotel.eyjar.is. Owned by *Hótel Þórshamar*, a small and welcoming guesthouse behind the hotel with sleeping-bag accommodation from ISK 2200 and made-up beds.

F Guesthouse Árný, Illugata 7, 900 Vestmannaeyjar, **T** 481 2082. Up the hill from the harbour towards the swimming pool and airport, a homely guesthouse with dorms, single and double rooms, and washing and cooking facilities. Cheaper sleeping-bag accommodation from ISK 1700.

F Guesthouse Erna, Kirkubæjarbraut 15, 900 Vestmannaeyjar, **T** 481 2112. Friendly guesthouse at the base of the lava flow with cooking facilities, about five to ten minutes from the harbour. Sleeping bag accommodation from ISK 2000.

F Guesthouse Heimir, Heiðarvegur 1, 900 Vestmannaeyjar, **T** 481 2929. Once the youth hostel, this large guesthouse has comfortable rooms, includes breakfast and has a huge mural on the outside wall. Friendly and cosy, sleeping-bag accommodation from ISK 1700.

Apartments

C Gisting, Kirkjuvegur 28, 900 Vestmannaeyjar, **T** 567 0790, jonbergur@isl.is. Apartment for rent in central Heimaey with daily and weekly rates. Perfect for exploring the island's volcanoes and walking trails, with a comfortable bed and small kitchen area.

Hostels and campsites

G Campsite, Herjólfsdalur, 900 Vestmannaeyjar, **T** 481 2915. Small camping area beside the golf course and cliffs where puffins burrow in the summer. Basic facilities consisting of a bathroom and a hut for shelter. ISK 700 per person.

Akureyri

Hotels and guesthouses

A Hótel Kea, Hafnarstræti 87-89, 600 Akureyri, **T** 460 2000, www.keahotels.is. *Map 5 detail, G3, p255* Large, smart, professional-class hotel with showers in each room and breakfast included. Sauna, satellite TV and all the mod cons you'd expect. The city's top hotel.

B Hótel Norðurland, Geislagata 7, 600 Akureyri, **T** 462 2600, www.keahotels.is. *Map 5 detail, E3, p255* One of the Keahotels chain, a modern business-class hotel in the very centre of Akureyri with a welcoming atmosphere.

C Hótel Björk, Hafnarstræti 67, 600 Akureyri, **T** 460 2000, www.keahotels.is. *Map 5 detail, H3, p255* Smaller sister hotel to

Kea with similar business-standard rooms and friendly staff. Björk means 'birch' in Icelandic – no connection with the singer.

D Guesthouse Akureyri, Hafnarstræti 104, 600 Akureyri, **T** 462 5588, www.gistiheimilid.net. *Map 5 detail, G3, p255* Pleasant, central guesthouse with 29 rooms and an upmarket atmosphere.

E Akur Inn, Brekkugata 27a , 600 Akureyri, **T** 461 2500, www.akurinn.is. *Map 5 detail, E2, p255* Homely guesthouse near the centre of town set in a beautiful house with good views over the islands of Eyjafjörður. Rooms can accommodate one to five people.

E Brekkusel, Byggðavegur 97, 600 Akureyri, **T** 461 2660, www.brekkusel.is. *Map 5 detail, F1, p255* Medium-sized guesthouse with a studio flat for hire, single and double rooms, and sleeping-bag accommodation. Family-style relaxed environment with kitchen facilities and a hot pot.

E Guesthouse Ás, Skipagata 4 and Hafnarstræti 77, 602 Akureyri, **T** 461 2248. *Map 5 detail, H3, p255* Two small guesthouses offering bed and breakfast in the centre of Akureyri with moderate-sized rooms, relaxed and friendly.

E Guesthouse Glerá, Glerá 2, 603 Akureyri, **T** 462 5723, www.glera2.is. A few minutes' drive from the centre. Previously a farm, the converted barn has great views of the surrounding countryside. Rooms are colourful and clean and have shared bathroom facilities. There's also a spacious living room, kitchen and balcony. Sleeping-bag accommodation for ISK 2000.

E Guesthouse Súlur, Þórunnarstræti 93 and Klettastígur 6, 600 Akureyri, **T** 461 1160, sulur@islandia.is. *Map 5 detail, H2 and E1, p255*

Large comfortable rooms in a guesthouse/small hotel at two different locations. With cooking facilities, laundry and breakfast room. Cheaper sleeping-bag accommodation is also available. Open 1 June to 31 August.

E Guesthouse Úllu, Langahlíð 6, 603 Akureyri, **T** 462 3472. *Map 5, A3, p255* Reasonably priced accommodation on the peaceful outskirts of Akureyri with sleeping-bag places from ISK 2100. If you don't have your own transport the bus from/to Reykjavík can stop here en route.

E Gula Villan, Þingvallastræti 14, 600 Akureyri, **T** 461 2860, gulavillan@nett.is. *Map 5 detail, G2, p255* Small, friendly and organized B&B with 10 rooms in central Akureyri with a kitchen.

E Hótel Edda, Eyralandsvegur 28, 600 Akureyri, **T** 461 1434, www.hoteledda.is. *Map 5 detail, F1, p255* Offering sleeping-bag accommodation from ISK 1000 as well as double, triple and single rooms, it's one of the Edda chain of basic countryside hotels throughout Iceland – boarding schools that become accommodation in the summer months. Good value but you'll need a car to reach it.

E Salka, Skipagata 1, 600 Akureyri, **T** 461 2340, salka@nett.is. *Map 5 detail, F3, p255* Three large rooms and a kitchen in this four-storey house in the centre of town. Sleeping-bag places or made-up beds.

E Sólgarður, Brekkagata 6, 600 Akureyri, **T** 461 1133, solgardar@ simnet.is. *Map 5 detail, E2, p255* Recommended pleasant and friendly budget guesthouse in the middle of Akureyri with a kitchen and lounge. Also offers sleeping-bag accommodation from ISK 1800.

Hostels and campsites

G Akureyri Youth Hostel, Stórholt 1, 603 Akureyri, **T** 462 3657, www.hostel.is. *Map 5, A3, p255* A 15-minute walk out of the city, the family which runs this small hostel is really friendly. Dorms, single and double rooms but make sure you reserve a room in advance as there's very little accommodation in this price bracket in the city.

G Húsabrekka Campsite, across the fjord from Akureyri on the eastern shore of Eyjafjörður, **T** 462 4921. Basic campsite with wonderful views, close to the road, about 6 km from Akureyri with caravan, cabin and camping accommodation.

Around Akureyri

Hotels

B Hotel Reynihlíð, Reynihlíð, 660 Mývatn, **T** 464 4170, www.reynihlid.is. The nicer of the two small hotels in Reynihlíð with a restaurant, bar and comfortable rooms. Next door is the reasonably priced, warm and cosy café, *Gamli Bærinn*. Car, bike and horse hire available. Open June to mid-September.

D Eldá Tourist Centre Campsite and Hotel, Reynihlíð, 660 Mývatn, **T** 464 4220, www.elda.is Small campsite by the lake and a small, relaxed hotel. Bring some insect repellent! B&B in the area can also be arranged as can most of the activities in the area including boating and cycling.

The islands of Eyjafjörður

Hotels

E The Brekka Restaurant , **T** 466 1751, brekkahrisey@isl.is.
Small restaurant offering standard B&B accommodation in twin
rooms with made-up beds or sleeping-bag accommodation.
Affords an impressive view of the midnight sun.

E-F Guesthouse Gullsól, 611 Grímsey, **T** 467 3114, grimsey@
ismennt.is. Small guesthouse with friendly personal service.

F Básar, Básum, 611 Grímsey, **T** 467 3103, sigrun@konica.is. The
largest of the two guesthouses, a warm family-run place offering
sleeping-bag accommodation from ISK 1700 and made-up beds.

G Hrísey Campsite, **T** 466 3012. Basic campsite perfect for
getting back to nature, no mod cons. They can also arrange
sleeping-bag accommodation in the local school in the summer.

Húsavík

Hotels

B Fosshotel Húsavík, Ketilsbraut 22, 640 Húsavík, **T** 464 1220,
www.fosshotel.is. Small professional hotel in the centre of town
with all mod cons and a beautiful view of the fjord. There's also a
bar and restaurant and breakfast is included.

D Árból guesthouse, Ásgarðsvegur 2, 640 Húsavík, **T** 464 2220,
www.simnet.is/arbol.   Small, comfortable guesthouse by a stream.
The house dates from 1903 and is warm, romantic and homely.

Eating and drinking

Reykjavík offers a range of different food from all over the world but best by far is the fish and the lamb. Around Lækjargata you'll find the tourist restaurants where there are 'all you can eat' fish buffets, puffin bonanzas and places to try the weird and wonderful.

Eating out is expensive but the standard is very high and places around Austurstræti are stylish and popular. Cheaper options can be found and there's a marked difference in price between restaurants with hip modern decor and starched white tablecloths and those that are more casual in look. Lunch starts at around 1300 and it can be difficult to find anywhere for breakfast before 1100. Dinner is served from around 1800 until 2200 and the majority of eateries are in 101 Reykjavík.

There are few places open later for dinner except at weekends when the *pylsur* (hotdog) stalls come out in force around Lækjartorg Square. Alcoholic drinks in the city are expensive in bars and restaurants but can otherwise be bought from the state controlled off-licences, *Vinbuðin*.

Eating codes

⑪	ISK 2600 and over
⑪	ISK 1300-2600
⑪	ISK 1300 and under

Prices given here are per head for two courses excluding drinks. Tips are always included. For meals costing upwards of ISK 1300 service is always included.

Icelandic cuisine is a matter of taste. On the one hand there is some of the best fresh fish you can buy on the planet as well as exquisite lamb; on the other you've got the dubious delights of *hákarl* (putrefied cubed sharkmeat) as well as *lundi* (puffin) and whale meat. Puffin tastes very rich and gamey, and the breasts are served either smoked or lightly grilled. Shark meat can be ordered as a starter in specialist Icelandic restaurants, but it's not a great idea as the flavour is noxious to say the least and will certainly spoil your meal. Some delicious specialities to look out for, though, are salmon, lamb, *skýr* (a thick, yoghurty dessert) and salt licorice.

Eating out in Reykjavík and Iceland is, in general, very expensive. If you're on a budget, the only way to keep the costs low is to cook for yourself or eat at the undistinguished snack bars. For somewhere really special, try the highly recommended *Siggi Hall*. There isn't a dress code as such but you will see a number of men in jackets and even ties at the smarter places.

! *Hákárl* and *brennivín* in combination are said to be a good hangover cure. It might be wiser to try one of the hot pots in a nearby thermal pool or buy a hangover remedy from the *10-11* store, though, as putrefied shark meat and potent rocket fuel aren't always the best combination.

Coffee makes Reykjavík go round. It's ground, high-quality and high-octane with enough caffeine to keep you up all day and night. Café society is alive and kicking in the city and most of the coffee shops mentioned here serve snacks and double up as bars in the evening. Thankfully there isn't a single Coffee Republic or Starbucks to date and you can spend an easy afternoon checking out the bizarre fashions and listening to the most recent Icelandic music with a large pot of coffee at your side for around ISK 200. Icelanders are reticent, though, and don't really engage in conversation with strangers when sober. They are riotous when drunk and ready to tell their unedited life story, but understandably quieter the next day. Most cafés open around 1100 and close at 0100 during the week and later on Friday and Saturday. The city doesn't wake up much before 1000 and cafés in general don't open their doors until a little later.

101 Reykjavík

Restaurants

♔♔♔ Apótek, Austurstræti 16, **T** 575 7900, www.veitingar.is. *Café-bar open from 1100, restaurant for dinner from 1800. Map 2, E3, p250* Fashionable restaurant serving fusion cuisine. *Apótek* used to be a pharmacy, hence the name, but now dispenses tongue-twisting goodies like Tahitian tuna tartar with wonton soup and a range of sushi instead of pills and potions. It's certainly the place to see and be seen, and is good for coffee and their extra special brownie with orange sorbet during the day. The separate bar-café menu is good value and equally delicious.

♔♔♔ Argentina, Barónsstígur 11a, **T** 551 9555, www.argentina.is. *Daily from 1800. Map 2, G8, p251* If you're looking for meat in this city, this is the place to visit. *Argentina* is a darkly seductive basement restaurant serving exceptional mouth-watering steaks

> ## Five of the weirdest Icelandic specialities

Hákarl As mentioned before, this is basically rotten shark meat cubed and served as a starter. The taste stays with you for far longer than you'd want, and the best way of losing it is by necking a shot of *brennivín*, a clear alcoholic spirit with a bit of a kick to it to say the least.

Pickled ram's testicles Often served pressed into a cake with garlic, as a jam or as a kind of pâté. It doesn't taste too bad if you don't think about it too much, particularly in the pâté form.

Cod chins or cheeks You might think this is a mistranslation when you see it on the menu, but the Icelanders often prefer to eat the meat from cod heads than the more traditional fillets. It's a delicacy and certainly nicer than sheep's head, also a national dish, originating from the days when it was necessary to eat everything available to stay alive.

Seabirds Take your pick from smoked puffin, guillemot and boiled fulmar's eggs – they have a slight oily flavour but can be delicious, especially as a starter. Beware if you're thinking of buying eggs from the market to cook yourself, though, as it's common for seabirds' eggs to contain half-hatched chicks.

Pylsur Not so much weird as weirdly popular, Icelandic hotdogs are a national dish of their own, frankfurter sausages smothered in mustard, ketchup, onions and anything else the vendor can get his hands on. They all taste very similar, but the stall by the harbour is supposed to be the best. Don't forget the mints afterwards.

of all description, specializing in beef. It's the winner of numerous accolades and is recommended.

🍴 **Austur Indía Félagið**, Hverfisgata 56, **T** 552 1630, www.austurindia.is. *Map 2, F7, p250* This upmarket Indian restaurant is not only the northernmost Indian restaurant in the world, it is one of the best in Europe. The cuisine looks, tastes and smells very authentic indeed and is very reasonably priced.

¶¶¶ **Brasserie Borg**, Pósthússtræti 11, Austurvöllur Square, **T** 551 1247, www.hotelborg.is. *Open for snacks all day, dinner 1800-2100. Map 2, E3, p250* As you'd expect, it's a dining experience at this art-deco hotel with a small menu featuring rainbow trout, lamb, lobster and reindeer, served in an environment that'll make you feel like a 1950s film star.

¶¶¶ **Café Opera**, Lækjargata 2, **T** 552 9499, www.cafeopera.is. *Daily 1800-0100, Fri-Sat 1800-0300, kitchen open to 2330, 0100 Fri-Sat. Map 2, E3, p250* Opera, as it's known to locals, is a traditional restaurant with a cosy antique atmosphere and excellent food including a 'hot rock special' where you can grill your own fish or steak at your table. They've also got an extensive wine list and serve Icelandic specials like guillemot and dolphin. One of the few places open past 2200, with a cosy wine bar upstairs.

¶¶¶ **Caruso**, Þingholtstræti 1, **T** 562 7335, www.caruso.is. *Daily 1130-2300. Map 2, E4, p250* Traditional Italian restaurant on the corner of Laugavegur with lunch specials, pizza and much more expensive meat dishes in an intimate, warm restaurant.

¶¶¶ **Einar Ben**, Veltusundi 1, **T** 511 5090, www.einarben.is. *Map 2, D2, p250* The place for fine dining. Set on the top floor of a 19th century timber house with soft lighting, drapes and chandeliers. Named after one of Iceland's most famous poets. The menu features contemporary Icelandic and international cuisine with á la carte and set menus. Relaxed and friendly atmosphere.

¶¶¶ **Humarhúsið Restaurant**, Amtmannsstígur 1, **T** 561 3303, www.humarhusid.is. *Daily 1100-2330. Map 2, E4, p250* 'The

Lobster House'. One of Reykjavík's finest seafood restaurants, specializing particularly in lobster and offering tempting dishes like pan-fried catfish with papaya salsa. The traditional wooden building adds to the intimate and warm atmosphere.

ⓘ **Iðnó**, Vonarstræti, **T** 562 9700 *Coffee shop open 1200-1800, restaurant open 1800-2200. Map 2, E3, p250* This elegant restaurant overlooks the pond and is in the oldest theatre in Iceland, which accounts for the antique feel. There's a small coffee shop on the first floor with the theatre while the restaurant is on the second and third floors. The restaurant serves traditional Icelandic seafood, game and meat dishes and has a reasonably priced á la carte menu.

ⓘ **Lækjarbrekka**, Bankastræti 2, **T** 551 4430, www.laekjarbrekka.is. *Daily 1100-2400. Map 2, E4, p250* Right next door to the tourist information centre, this is the place for an authentic tourist experience, including the fish buffet and puffin party. It's one of the oldest houses in Reykjavík, built in 1834, with a well-preserved and distinguished interior, but you'll find few Icelanders eating here. Fish buffet from 1800 in summer.

ⓘ **La Primavera**, Austurstræti 9, 2nd floor, **T** 561 8555, www.laprimavera.is. *Mon-Fri 1200- 1430, Sun-Thu 1100-2300, Fri-Sat 1800-2330. Map 2, D3, p250* Upmarket Italian affair, with a stylish and modern interior and expensive and delicious pasta. Attracts a young, fashionable clientele.

ⓘ **Maru**, Aðalstræti 12, **T** 511 4440, www.maru.is. *Map 2, D2, p250* *Maru* offers upmarket Japanese and Thai cuisine including sushi, curry, Miso soup, noodles, *yakitori* (Japanese kebabs) and a range of other enchanting dishes. There's a sake bar in the cellar.

ⓘ **Naustið**, Vesturgata 6-8, **T** 554 0500, www.naustid.is *Daily from 1800. Map 2, C1, p250* The oldest restaurant in the city with antique-style decor, intimate booths and cheerful staff. In a classy atmosphere you'll be served mainly Icelandic dishes like grilled whale steak with wildberry sauce, guillemot, smoked lamb and the house speciality of seafood gratin.

¶¶¶ **Þrir Frakkar**, Baldursgata 14, **T** 552 3939, www.3frakkar.com. *Mon-Thu 1100- 2300, Sat-Sun 1800-2330. Map 2, H5, p251* Popular Icelandic seafood restaurant specializing in local specialities such as whale meat or puffin. The name is an Icelandic play on words, meaning both 'three Frenchmen' and 'three trenchcoats'. Small, intimate and very Icelandic. Free wine if you have to wait for a table. Recommended if you like fish.

¶¶¶ **Siggi Hall**, Þórsgata 1, **T** 511 6677, www.siggihall.is. *Daily from 1800. Map 2, G5, p251* Next to the *Óðinsvé Hotel* is Reykjavík's finest restaurant. *Siggi Hall* is known to Icelanders all over for his regular weekly TV show and to even more, now that he's opened up a city centre restaurant, for his shellfish soufflé and *bacalao* (salt cod). It's a stylish and relaxed place to dine, particularly good for its Icelandic fish, game and lamb.

¶¶¶ **Skólabrú**, Pósthússtræti 17, **T** 562 4455. *Daily from 1800. Map 2, E3, p250* Old timber house from the turn of the century housing an exclusive, classy restaurant. *Skólabrú* is very tasteful and serves gourmet food, ranging from flambéed lobster tails to champagne sorbets, and specializing in fish and international cuisine. Attracts an older clientele.

¶¶¶ **Tjarnarbakkinn**, Vonarstræti 3, **T** 562 9700, www.idno.is. *Map 2, E2, p250* Known in English as *The Lake Front Restaurant*, it is housed in a historic building, above the Iðnó theatre, so it's a good place to go beforehand. It serves authentic Icelandic cuisine and has good views out over the pond.

¶¶¶ **Við Tjörnina**, Templarasund 3, **T** 551 8666, www.islandia.is/~vidtjornina. *Daily 1200-2300. Map 2, E3, p250* With a prime location down towards the pond, this is another specialist seafood restaurant but this time with a French twist. They have a particularly large selection of wines and a daily specials menu starting from ISK 3100 in an intimate historic restaurant.

¶¶¶ **Red River Steakhouse**, Rauðararstigur 37, **T** 562 6766, www.raudara.is. A cosy, intimate atmosphere in the building which used to be Reykjavík's first brewery. Solid wooden tables, candles and Icelandic cuisine including whale, puffin and reindeer, as well as more conservative choices, make this place a recommended choice.

¶¶ **Asía**, Laugavegur 10, **T** 562 6210. *Daily 1200-2200. Map 2, E6, p250* Oriental restaurant serving a wide array of Chinese-style fish, prawn, beef and chicken dishes in a large restaurant on the main shopping street. Lunch is a bargain ISK 950 for three courses and you can expect to pay about ISK 1400 for dinner.

¶¶ **Café Victor**, Hafnarstræti 1-3, **T** 561 9555, www.cafevictor.is. *Daily from 1100. Map 2, D3, p250* Casual bistro-bar serving Mediterranean food, sandwiches for under ISK 1000 and a small tourist menu. Soup of the day with a fish main course costs around ISK 1790. It's also a nice place to stop for coffee. Large screen for sports fans, turns into a nightclub in the evening.

¶¶ **Enrico's**, Laugavegi 3, **T** 552 0077, www.enricos.is. *Map 2, E5, p250* Classy new restaurant and café on the main street, with leather sofas and an arty feel. Special lunch menus with light snacks or more substantial tasty meals. Good service, but maintains a relaxed atmosphere.

¶¶ **Hornið**, Hafnarstræti 15, **T** 551 3340, www.hornid.is. *Daily 1100-2330. Map 2, D3, p250* French and Mediterranean food served up in a classy environment with marble tables and lots of foliage. It's a popular place for coffee and cakes during the day as well as pan-fried arctic char, pizza and seafood later on.

¶¶ **Indókína**, Laugavegur 19, **T** 552 2399. *For lunch and evening meals until 2200. Map 2, F7, p250* Small Oriental specialist with reasonable set lunches for around ISK 745 for five small courses and set dinner for ISK 1350-1500. It's one of many similar oriental places to eat out in the city.

¶¶ **Kaffisetrið**, Laugavegur 103, **T** 552 5444. *Daily 1000-2330. Map 2, G8, p251* Small Icelandic-Thai restaurant with breakfast, lunch offers and dinners of reasonably priced Thai food and Icelandic fish, lamb and pork. Also serves dinner after 2200.

¶¶ **Kína Húsið**, Lækjargata 8, **T** 551 1014. *Mon-Thu 1130-1400 and 1730-2200, Fri till 2300. Sat 1700-2300, Sun 1700-2200. Map 2, E3, p250* Chinese food with cheaper lunchtime specials at ISK 750-850 for a number of courses. Warm, hospitable environment where most people choose to eat in rather than take away.

¶¶ **Pasta Basta**, Klapparstígur 38, **T** 511 2238. *Daily 1200-1400 and from 1800. Map 2, F6, p250* Small Italian restaurant popular with young Reykjavíkurs, serving particularly good traditional Italian and Mediterranean dishes. Lunch specials are around ISK 1200.

¶¶-¶ **First Vegetarian**, also known as *A Naestu Grosum*, Laugavegur 20b, **T** 552 8410, www.anaestugrosum.is. *Mon-Sat 1130-2200, Sun 1800-2200. Map 2, F7, p250* Homely café-style dining in a restaurant serving Indian and Italian specials as well as soup, sandwiches, coffee and cake throughout the day for lunch and supper. There's also a variety of organic beer, wine and juice

Café society
Reykjavík is fuelled by caffeine and the city's many stylish cafés are always buzzing.

and it's all served in a welcoming, good-value first-floor restaurant looking out onto the main shopping street. Recommended.

₩-₩ Rossopomodro, Laugavegur 40a, **T** 561 0500, www.rosso pomodoro.is. *Map 2, F7, p250* One of the best Italian restaurants in town with a cosy atmosphere and reasonable prices. Pizzas are cooked in a big woodfire oven and portions are generous. Despite being fairly new on the scene, it already has a devoted clientele.

₩ Baejarins Beztu, corner of Tryggvagata and Pósthússtræti. *Map 2, D3, p250* Reykjavík's original hotdog kiosk has become something of an insitution, despite its uninspiring location in a car park facing the harbour. The hotdogs (*pylsur*) comes with mustard, ketchup and raw and fried onions and are very tasty.

₩ Galileo Pizzeria, Hafnarstræti 1-3, **T** 552 9500, www.galileo.is. *Daily 1130-2330. Map 2, D3, p250* Smart pizzeria serving a range of international foods from grilled lamb, salmon and lobster to foal and lima beans. Fairly stylish and more expensive for meat, which costs around ISK 1700, than for fish and pizza.

¶ **Jómfrúin**, Lækjargata 4, **T** 557 0100, www.mmedia.is/jomfruin.
Daily 1100-2200, 20 Apr-20 Sep. Map 2, E3, p250 Danish
open-sandwich restaurant with a bistro feel. Beef and salmon
sandwiches start at around ISK 1150. Occasionally hosts
mid-afternoon jazz recitals in summer.

¶ **Shalimar**, Austurstræti 4, **T** 551 0292, www.shalimar.is.
*Mon-Thu 1130-2200, Fri-Sat 1130-2300, Sun 1700-2200. Map 2, D2,
p250* It's a bit unusual to be served lamb madras by a fair-haired,
blue-eyed Icelandic waitress, but that's what you get here. It's one
of the cheapest places to get a filling meal and is popular with the
locals. Lunch deals are even cheaper than evening meals.

Cafés and bistros

¶¶ **Kaffi Sólon** Bankastræti 7a, **T** 562 3232, www.solon.is. *Map 2,
E5, p251* Always popular and generally packed, with fuky artwork
and seats spilling out onto the street. Tasty, filling and reasonably
priced food. Friendly, relaxing atmosphere with a bar upstairs and a
disco later on. Turns into a nightclub at weekends.

¶¶ **Postbarinn**, Pósthússtræti 13, **T** 562 7830, www.postbarinn.is.
Sun-Thu 1130-0100, Fri-Sat 1200-0300. Map 2, E3, p251 In the heart
of the city looking out onto the cathedral and Austurvöllur Square.
Postbarinn is comfortable and laid-back bar-bistro serving good
value and tasty food.

¶¶ **Vegamót**, Vegamótastígur 4, **T** 551 3040, www.vegamot.is.
*Mon-Thu 1100-0100, Fri-Sat 1100-0500, Sun 1200-0100. Map 2, E5,
p250* Just off Laugavegur, a stylish and popular bistro-bar with
international cuisine and outdoor patio filled with chattering people
on a nice weekend. Serves club sandwiches for around ISK 800 and
the catch of the day plus a beer costs ISK 1490. Reykjavík's young
and beautiful dine and drink here at weekends. Recommended.

★ **Places for an early breakfast**

Best
- Hotel Borg, p116
- Café Paris, p149
- Grái Kötturinn, p150
- Kaffivagninn, p150
- Kaffitar, p150

¶¶-¶ **Café Paris**, Austurstræti 14, **T** 551 1020, www.cafeparis.is. *Sun-Thu 0800- 2400, Fri-Sat 1000-0100. Map 2, E3, p250* With the best view of Austurvöllur Square and often spilling out into the street, *Café Paris* is a refined café doubling as a bar with a relaxed Sunday-morning atmosphere. Popular for coffee and ice creams.

¶ **Ari í Ögri**, Ingólfsstræti 3, **T** 551 9660. *Sun-Thu 1100-0100, Fri-Sat 1130-0300. Map 2, E4, p250* Just off Laugavegur, this small pub serves snacks as well as hearty all-day breakfasts. Sandwiches start at about ISK 500 and fish at ISK 1500. It's neither classy nor trendy like the majority of the city's bars and restaurants, but the food is good value.

¶ **Café Cultura**, Hverfisgata 18, **T** 530 9314, www.cultura.is. *Map 2, E4, p250* On the ground floor of the Intercultural Centre, the café provides a forum for cultural activities and artistic talent. During the day it's a hangout for actors from the National Theatre, just across the road. Great for a coffee and a chat, or try the multi-ethnic food. Concerts and theme nights such as Salsa or Tango.

¶ **Café Garðurinn**, Klappurstígur 37, **T** 561 2345. *Mon-Tue, Thu-Fri 1100-2000, Wed 1100-1800, Sat 1200-1700, Sun closed. Map 2, F6, p250* Small vegetarian café/restaurant with a daily selection of home-cooked vegetarian specialities, soup, sandwiches, coffee, tea and cakes.

¶ **Gott í Goginn**, Laugavegur 2a, **T** 552 4444. *Mon-Thu 1030-2000, Fri-Sat 1030-1900, closed Sun. Map 2, E5, p250* Meaning 'good in the beak', this small deli/take away snack bar on Laugavegur sells pizza, pasta, Mexican food and sandwiches at reasonable prices. Cheap food on the go.

¶ **Grái Kötturinn**, Hverfisgata 16a, **T** 551 1544. *Mon-Fri 0700- 1700, Sat 0900-1700. Map 2, E5, p250* A bohemian 1950s-style diner with bookshop chic. The *Grey Cat*, named after a cat that once lived in the building, is run by artists. There's a mixture of books to look through while you're tucking into large plates of hangover-style fry-ups and pancakes, costing around ISK 1000.

¶ **Kaffitar**, Bankastræti 8 , **T** 511 4540. *Mon-Sat 0730-1800, Sun 1000-1800. Map 2, F6, p250* The closest thing to a *Starbucks* in the city with a wide range of different coffees and other branches at the nearby malls. The saving grace is many and varied continental breakfast foods, bagels and cakes, all at reasonable prices.

¶ **Kaffivagninn**, Grandargarði 10, **T** 551 5932. *Daily 0730-1800. Map 2, A1, p250* A 10-15 minute walk from the centre of town, the *Coffee Wagon* overlooks the old harbour and you can watch the small fishing boats come and go. It's a bit of a walk, but worth it. It's a lovely small diner-style café to relax in away from the trendy crowds and more of a local's haunt than many of the others. If you're an early bird, this one's for you.

¶ **Kaffi Hljómalind**, Laugavegur 21. *Map 2, F7, p250* This cosy café with painted windows is right on the main street and perfect for people-watching. It's run by a non-for-profit organization and serves a tasty selection of organic and fair-trade products.

Kaffi Reykjavík, Vesturgata 2, **T** 552 3030, www.kaffireykjavik.is. *Mon-Thu 1130-0100, Fri-Sun 1200-0400. Map 2, C2, p250* A vast pub and one of the few places where the less -fashionable hang out at. There's a fish buffet daily from 1800 and alcohol promotions. Live music most evenings, generally golden-oldie cover bands with mullets (haircuts, not fish). There's also an ice bar, entry ISK 1300 including free drink, but don't expect to find any locals here.

Kofi Tómasar Frænda, Laugavegur 2, **T** 551 1855. *Mon-Thu 1000-0100, Fri-Sat till late. Map 2, E5, p250* Cosy basement café on the main shopping street serving snacks, coffee and cake during the day and into the evening. There's also a good supply of *Hello!* magazines and it's a welcoming place on a slow Sunday afternoon.

Mokka Kaffi, Skólavörðustígur 3a, **T** 552 1174, www.mokka.is. *Mon-Sat 0930-2330, Sun 1400-2330. Map 2, G6, p251* The oldest café in town, dating from 1958, *Mokka* is an intimate art gallery/café serving the best waffles in town. A quiet refuge popular with the locals.

Oliver, Laugavegur 20a, **T** 562 5059. *Sun-Thu 1000-0100, Fri-Sat 1000-0400. Map 2, F7, p250* Light, stylish café serving snacks and Italian food. There's also a particularly good wine list. The café is open for sandwiches for around ISK 800, and coffee and cake during the afternoon, then it turns into a bar in the evening. Slow service.

Ömmukaffi, Austurstræti 20, **T** 552 9680. *Mon-Fri 0930-1800, Sat 1200-2200, Sun closed. Map 2, E3, p250* Very cheap café run by the YMCA serving sandwiches, pastries, coffee and cakes.

Ráðhúskaffi, city hall. *Map 2, E3, p250* Snacks, sandwiches and cakes. Lovely views out over the town pond, great place for coffee on a rainy day. Free internet if you buy a drink.

Old Harbour

Restaurants

¶¶¶ Tveir Fiskar, Geirsgata 9, **T** 511 3474, www.restaurant.is.
*Lunch Mon-Fri 1200-1400, dinner daily from 1800. Map 2, B2,
p250* Refined Icelandic fish restaurant over- looking the harbour.
Specialities include oyster soup, smoked puffin with pear
marmalade and caviar. You can also try caviar, dolphin or whale
steak. A high-quality modern gourmet affair with a feng-shuied
interior and stylish bar.

¶ Krúa Thai, Tryggvagata 14, **T** 561 0039, www.kruathai.is.
*Mon-Fri 1130-2130, Sat 1200-2130, Sun 1700-2130. Map 2, C2,
p250* Small Thai restaurant serving deep-fried fish, shrimps, chicken
and all that you'd expect at unbelievable prices for this city. There's
an even cheaper lunchtime special Monday to Friday costing ISK 590
for three courses.

¶ Seagreifinn, Verbúð 8, **T** 553 1500. *Daily 0800-1800. Map 2,
B2, p250* Run by three local fishermen including the 'sea baron'
himself, this is actually a fish shop with a couple of wooden
benches outside. The charming harbour setting and truly rustic feel
make it a good, cheap spot for lunch. Try the delicious lobster soup
for ISK 650 or a kebab made of whale, cod or eel.

Cafés

¶¶-¶ Pizza 67, Tryggvagata 26, **T** 561 9900. *Sun-Thu 1130-2200,
Fri-Sat 1130-2300. Map 2, C2, p250* Full of teenagers, a reasonable
chain of pizza cafés emblazoned with 1960s slogans. Discount of
20% for students with a valid ISIC card.

Öskjuhlíð Hill

Restaurants

⦙⦙⦙ Perlan Öskjuhlíð, 105 Reykjavík, **T** 562 0200,
www.perlan.is. *Daily from 1900. Map 1, F5, p248* Highly rated
Icelandic restaurant serving meat and seafood to distinguished
diners with a slowly revolving floor and beautiful views of the city.
Serves lobster, veal, beef, lamb and even grilled reindeer. Almost
prohibitively expensive even by Icelandic standards, the most
luxurious dining experience to be had. An average meal costs
ISK 5000-5500 per person.

Cafés

⦙⦙-⦙ Kaffee Nauthóll, Nauthólsvegur, Nauthólsvík Beach, **T** 562
9910. *Mon-Fri 1100-2300, Sat-Sun 1000-2300, food served till
2000. Map 1, H5, p248* Take bus No 7 to Perlan and walk down the
hill or stay on the bus until *Hótel Loftleiðir* and walk down the path
to the beach. A little out of town but well worth a visit. The only
turf-roofed café in town, down by the beach and cosy and warm
inside. The slabs of chocolate cake are delicious as are the range of
seafood salads costing ISK 800-1500.

Hafnarfjörður

⦙⦙⦙ Fjörukráin, Viking Village, Strandgata 50a, 220 Hafnarfjörður,
T 565 1891, www.fjorukrain.is. *Sun-Thu 1200-0100, Fri-Sat
1200-0300. Map 4, E3, p254* Eat as much as you can in the Viking
hall of *Fjörukráin*. The food, including lamb, schnapps and *skyr*,
is exceptional and a banquet of traditional fare costs ISK 4600
including drinks and some great Viking and Valkyrie impersonations.

¶¶ **A Hansen**, Vesturgata 4, 220 Hafnarfjörður, **T** 565 1130, www.ahansen.is. *Map 4, D3, p254* Low-key restaurant in one of the oldest houses in Hafnarfjörður, built in 1880. Serves tasty nouvelle cuisine and can organize transport so you don't have to worry about driving home.

Vestmannaeyjar (Westman Islands)

¶¶ **Café Maria**, Skólavegur 1, **T** 481 3160. *Daily 1100-2330*. Classy restaurant serving puffin, Italian food and a wide range of drinks. Undoubtedly the most stylish place to eat on Heimaey.

¶¶ **Fjolan**, Vestmannabraut 28, **T** 481 2900. In the same building as *Hotel Þórshamar* (see p130), *Fjola* (The Violet) serves seasonal dishes specialising in fowl, meat and seefood, according to season.

¶¶ **Lanterna**, Bárustígur 11, **T** 481 3393. *Daily 1100-2230*. Cosy Italian-Icelandic restaurant with excellent fish, puffin and enormous pizzas. It's decorated with photographs recalling Heimaey's fishing history and has a charming atmosphere.

¶¶ **Lundinn**, Kirkuvegur 21, **T** 481 1426. *From 1100*. Smart pub serving all kinds of snacks, pizza and more substantial fish and meat dishes.

¶¶ **Pizza 67**, Heiðavegur 5, **T** 481 1567. *Sun-Thu 1130-2200, Fri-Sat 1130-2300*. Another of the chain, this time in a small cosy pub sheltered from the elements with reasonably priced pizzas and student discounts.

¶ **Bakery and Konditori**, Kökuhús, Bárustígur 7. *Daily 1100-1700*. Small smart bakery with a café serving coffee, reasonably priced sandwiches and baked goods.

Akureyri

¶¶¶ Fiðlarinn, Skipagata 14, **T** 462 7100, www.fidlarinn.is. *Daily from 1800. Map 5 detail, F4, p255* Meaning 'the Fiddler', this upmarket French restaurant offers various daily set menus and a plush interior all set for fine dining.

¶¶¶ Friðrik V Brasserie, Strandgata 7, 2nd floor, **T** 461 5775, www.fridrikv.is. *Tue-Sun from 1800, closed Mon. Map 5 detail, E4, p255* Elegant and polished French restaurant with a stylish interior and delicious lamb. Recommended.

¶¶¶ La Vita e Bella, Hafnarstræti 92, **T** 461 5858, www.bautinn.is. *Daily from 1800. Map 5 detail, G3, p255* Large, welcoming Italian restaurant with good service and a relaxed environment.

¶¶¶ Rósagarðurinn, Hafnarstræti 87-80, **T** 460 2017, www.keahotels.is. *Map 5 detail, G3, p255* The 'Rose Garden' restaurant at *Hotel Kea* offers Icelandic cuisine and specially chosen wines to complement your food.

¶¶ Bláa Kannan Café, Hafnarstræti 92, **T** 461 4600. *Daily 0800-2300. Map 5 detail, F3, p255* Lovely large open café with modern art on the walls and mouth-watering cakes, filled croissants, and soup and pasta lunches. Open from 0800 and a perfect place for a continental breakfast.

¶¶ Café Amour, Ráðhústorgi 9, **T** 461 3030 *Daily 1100-2300. Map 5 detail, F3, p255* Relaxed wine bar/café with cream leather chairs, cocktails and light bar snacks, and seafood soup and salads.

¶¶ Greifinn, Glerágata 20, **T** 460 1600, www.greifinn.is. *Daily 1100-2330. Map 5, A4, p255* Italian-style restaurant that's perennially popular for its reasonably priced meals and family atmosphere. The fish is particularly recommended.

🍴 **Kaffi Akureyri**, Strandgata 7, **T** 461 3999, www.kaffiakyreyri.is. *Map 5 detail, E4, p255* A pleasant café-bar offering cakes and a variety of snacks. The back room turns into a popular disco at weekends and attracts a late-twenties crowd.

🍴 **Karolína**, Þingvallastræti, **T** 461 2755, www.karolina.is. *Mon-Thu 1130-0100, Fri-Sat 1130-0300, Sun 1400-0100. Restaurant open daily from 1800 in Summer, Tue-Fri in Winter. Map 5 detail, G2, p255* Small, arty and warm café and restaurant with modern European fusion food, snacks, beer and wine. The restaurant is more expensive but worth it. Jazz recitals every Thursday in summer and occasional art exhibitions add to the bohemian vibe.

🍴 **Tikk Takk Takeaway**, Raðhústorg, **T** 461 1300. *Mon-Thu 1130-2030, Fri 1130-0500, Sat 1700-0500, Sun 1700-2030. Map 5 detail, F3, p255* Range of well-priced fast food from pizza to sandwiches, Indian, Mexican and Chinese food. The added bonus is that it's open very late on a Friday and Saturday night if you're hungry on your way home.

For many people, Reykjavík's nightlife is the main reason for coming to this cold and windswept spot in the first place. It feels a bit odd compared to clubbing in other European destinations, particularly given the size of the city, but just as the country is geologically young and dynamic, the nightlife is too. It has had a lot of publicity in the last few years, causing some to find it a little over-hyped: it's certainly not like the nightlife you'd find in London or New York, but for a town this size it holds its own with over 120 bars and clubs.

Friday and Saturday nights are the wildest nights here, and that means serious clubbing from around 2400 to 0800 in the morning. The bars and clubs don't really fill up until after midnight. Those drinking in the bars and cafés before midnight are mainly tourists as the expense of drinking all night forces many of the locals to drink heavily at home before heading into town. Then to round it all off when the bars and clubs have closed, head for Austurvöllur Square where people tend to hang around. Coffee and lots of it are the order of the day on a Sunday.

The long summer days and yawning winter nights give a whole new twist to the concept of partying till dawn. Follow the crowd for a lively night; it's typical for bars to stay open as long as people are still drinking at the weekends, or alternatively close if no one's around. Music-wise you'll find a little bit of nearly everything in the city, from golden oldies to innumerable DJ sets and a few retro bars, although there isn't an abundance of rap or ethnic music.

Icelandic bands play at *Gaukur á Stöng* during the week and cafés push the ethereal sound of Sigur Rós during the day. Start your pub crawl at the corner of Bankastræti and Ingólfsstræti and head down the streets towards Austurvöllur Square. The bars and clubs noted below are primarily active in the evenings, but don't neglect the cafés (see p148) which are nearly all open as bars in the evening. DJ sets are popular at weekends at *Sirkus*, *Kaffeebarinn*, *Hverfisbarinn*, *Thorvaldsen* and any number of other places across the town. They're ever so slightly subdued during the week and very upbeat at the weekend and entry is generally free.

Reykjavíkurs have only had legal access to beer since 1989 and there are many unusual things about drinking in the city even today. In common with other Scandinavian countries, alcohol is state-controlled, expensive and, outside of bars and restaurants, can only be bought from the *Vinbuðin* shops. The closest one to the centre is on Austurstræti. This may go some to explaining why Icelanders don't go in for social drinking – getting sozzled is the order of the day. Pick up a copy of *The Grapevine*, www.grapevine.is, to see what's on.

101 Reykjavík

Bars and pubs

Ari í Ögri, Ingólfsstræti 3, **T** 551 9660. *Sun-Thu 1100-0100, Fri-Sat 1130-0300. Map 2, E4, p250* Small pub serving a wide selection of speciality beverages. There's live acoustic music every weekend.

Bar 11, Laugavegur 11, **T** 511 1180. *Map 2, E5, p250* This is the place to hang out with the rock'n'roll crowd of Reykjavík. With live classic or modern rock, DJs and jukebox music. Many of Iceland's rock bands are regulars here, including Krummi from the band Mínus. Screenings of cult films on Sundays. Make sure you try the *Brennivín*.

Bar 22, Laugavegur 22, **T** 517 5522. *Map 2, F6, p250* Downstairs there's a decent bistro while on the middle floor there's a dance floor. It's open late and a good place for those who want to sit and chat with a less trendy crowd. Gay friendly.

Café Rósenberg, Lækjargata 2, **T** 551 8008. *Map 2, E3, p250* The closest thing that Reykjavík has to a jazz club, with old instruments on the walls and live jazz or blues. People come here to listen to music and chat rather than to dance.

Dillon, Laugavegur 30, **T** 511 2400. *Sun-Thu 1300-0100. Fri-Sat 1300-1300. Map 2, F6, p250* Housed in a cosy wooden house, this is the closest thing you'll find to an English pub, with a nice beer garden out the back. It's busy even during the week when many places are empty. The resident DJ on Saturday is the grandmother of Icelandic rock star Andrea Jonsdottir.

The Dubliner, Hafnarstræti, **T** 511 3233. *Map 2, D3, p250* Despite, or perhaps because of, its reputation for being the most haunted pub in Reykjavík, the *Dubliner* is a popular Irish bar which pulls a decent pint of Guinness and has a good selection of whisky.

Hressingarskálinn, Austurstraeti 20, www.hresso.is. *Map 2, F5, p250* One of Reykjavík's oldest establishments, now under new management. Large L-shaped coffee house with an international atmosphere, board games and books. After 2300 at weekends the beat kicks in and things start rockin'.

Hverfisbarinn, Hverfisgata 20, **T** 511 6700, www.hverfisbarinn.is. *Sun-Thu 1130-0100, Fri-Sat 1130-0400. Map 2, E6, p250* Trendy café-bar-bistro with white leather sofas, minimalist decor, style magazines and a relaxing atmosphere. Things get a little more upbeat at the weekends with DJ sets and dancing.

Kaffibarinn, Bergstaðstræti 1, **T** 551 1588. *1100-0500. Map 2, F5, p250* One of Reykjavík's hippest hangouts for artists and musicians. Blur's Damon Albarn has a stake in this small corrugated-iron-clad two-storey bar and it's the place to spot the celebs when they're in town. It's laid-back and inviting, though, without a hint of snobbery. The old sofas and tables upstairs add a touch of bohemian glamour. Blend in with trainers, retro t-shirts and cords, and look out for Björk – this is her favourite bar.

Kaffi Brennslann, Posthússtræti 9, **T** 561 3600, www.brennslan.is. *Mon-Thu 1100-0100, Fri 1100-0300, Sat 1200-0300, Sun 1400-0100. Map 2, E3, p250* Laid-back, warm café-bar attracting a range of people. Sandwiches cost around ISK 800-1000. In the evenings try any one of a huge array of beers and relax amid the twinkling fairy lights. A great place to start your evening.

Kaffi Sólon, Bankastræti 7a, **T** 5623232, www.solon.is. *Map 2, E5, p250* With the *Red Room* club upstairs and a spacious, arty café downstairs, this is more of a well-groomed place than some of the others, filled with perfectly sleek blondes and a designer-clad mid- to late-twenties crowd.

Nellys Café, Þingholtsstræti 2, **T** 562 1250, www.nellys.is. *Map 2, E4, p250* Pulls the cheapest pints in town (ISK 450) and attracts seasoned drinkers during the week. At weekends there are often cover bands, attracting a younger crowd; there's a large dancefloor upstairs. Mixed gay and straight.

The bar to be in
*Reykjavik is full of hip bars and cafés and none
more so than Kaffeebarinn, here on the right.*

Oliver, Laugavegur 20 a, **T** 562 5059. *Map 2, F7, p250* One of the hottest places in town at the moment. Ultra chic and always crowded, usually has a large queue after 1100, especially at weekends. During the day it's a popular bar-bistro and one of the few places that opens early for breakfast or coffee.

Ölstofan, Vegamótastíg 4, **T** 552 4687. *Map 2, F6, p250* With a reputation for being the hangout for intellectuals in Reykjavík, this place attracts icelandic actors, TV personalities and musicians. There's no dancing, but plenty of smoking and drinking.

Prikið, Bankastræti 12, **T** 551 3366. *Map 2, F6, p250* The oldest place to party, *Prikið* means 'the stick' and is a fetchingly small and cosy place, ideal for starting your evening. Expect everyone from the young and hip to old men reading newspapers in the corner. Standing room only at weekends.

Thorvaldsen Bar, Austurstræti 10, T 511 1413, www.thorvalsden.is. *Map 2, E3, p250* A sleek, upwardly mobile place which spills into Austurvöllur Square on a sunny day with laid-back beats and a range of Thai, American and European snacks. It's light and hip with a minimalist interior and, bizarrely, a model of a small breast on the bookshelf, nothing to do with the strip club next door. Smart dress at weekends.

Bars and clubs

Vegamót, Vegamotastig 4, **T** 511 3040, www.vegamot.is. *Map 2, E/F5, p250* Elegant bar-bistro with two floors where . As the night progresses the atmosphere starts to change and the crowd with it as Vegamót evolves into a wild nightclub where Iceland's best DJ's turn their tricks in a non-stop party.

Clubs

Gaukur á Stöng, Tryggvagata 22, **T** 551 1556, www.gaukurinn.is. *Sun-Thu 2000- 0100, Fri-Sat 2000 till as late as the party's still going. Live bands around ISK 500. Map 2, D3, p250* Don't even bother to try pronouncing this name – it's virtually impossible to get your tongue round it. Reykjavíkurs call it *gaukurinn* and it's a dingy club that is home to young Icelandic bands. There are special nights of rock, pop, techno and hip-hop and it's really popular with the locals.

Glaumbar, Tryggvagata 22, **T** 552 6868, www.glaumbar.is. *Map 2, D3, p250* Sports bar with a big screen where you can watch sport until your hearts content. It's one of the few places in Reykjavík that's managed to get the barfly culture going. Open until five, and has a reputation for late night partying.

Grand Rokk , Smiðjustígur 6. *Map 2, E6, p250* One of the main venues for live music. This is the best place if you want something heavy metal and Gothic, with the occasional bit of rock'n'roll thrown in too.

NASA, Austurvöllur Sq, **T** 511 1313, www.nasa.is. *Fri-Sat 2200 onwards. ISK 1000. Map 2, E3, p250* NASA has lots of space and it's possible to see heavy metal acts during the week and shimmy to the most current disco and dance tunes at the weekend. It's easily the best place if you're looking for dance music.

Pravda, Austurstræti 22, **T** 552 9222, www.pravda.is. *Map 2, E3, p250* During the day *Pravda* is all chocolate and tan leather, Sunday supplements and relaxing music. At night it becomes a club playing disco/pop/dance, home to any kind of attrie from from the punky to the sleek and well groomed. Not as classy as *NASA*, though . Occasional live jazz or reggae.

Rex Bar, Austurstræti 9, **T** 552 5599, www.rex.is. *Map 2, E3, p250* Trendy London-style club with a cool interior and a great selection of wine.

Sirkus, Klapparstígur 31. *Map 2, E6, p250* A little like a beach hut from the outside, *Sirkus* is a hip hang-out with palm trees painted on the wall, a kitsch interior and laid-back retro, indie and hip-hop music. Popular with the arts, music and gay scene, expect the unexpected from topless lesbian dancing to more general madness. No entry fee, live music/DJs three times a week, beer ISK 550.

Despite its size, Reykjavík has a thriving arts scene and you should always be able to find something interesting to do or see. Much of the arts season is focused on the winter as Reykjavíkurs make use of the sunlight when it's there to spend time outdoors. This means that the National Theatre is in recess during the summer – when most tourists are here.

Icelanders visit the cinema more times per person than any other nationality, around five times a year, and you'll find a number of cinemas in the city centre. Films are shown in the original language with Icelandic subtitles.

It's contemporary music, above all, that is the live current running through the city all year round. Sung in both English and Icelandic, it fuses with the nightlife as one of the most popular attractions of the city. The city hosts yearly music, film and cultural festivals towards the end of the summer, see Festivals on p178. Daily events are advertised in the national newspapers, *Morgunblaðið* and *DV*, and for those not reading Icelandic the tourist office and youth hostel both have daily lists of what's on and where.

Cinema

Unfortunately, Reykjavík's cinemas conform to an international model – blockbusters and Hollywood releases are the standard fodder even in the country with more cinema-goers per head than any other. If you're lucky enough to track down any independent or art-house movies, the chances are that they'll be in the original language with Icelandic subtitles. On the plus side, check out Reykjavík's shops for Icelandic art-house films subtitled in English to take home with you. These are rarely available abroad. Foreign feature films cost ISK 800 in any cinema in Iceland. Check the local newspapers or at the tourist office for what's on and where. The daily free paper *Morgunbalðið* has cinema listings in English. To catch up on the latest film action in Iceland, see www.icelandic filmcentre.is. The website www.whatson.is is also useful.

There are six cinemas in Reykjavík which mainly show American movies in English with subtitles. **Háskólabió**, Hagatorg, 107 Reykjavík, **T** 530 1919, www.haskolabio.is. *Map 1, F1, p248*. **Regnboginn**, Hverfisgata 54, 101 Reykjavík, **T** 551 9000, www.www.regnboginn.is. *Map 2, F7, p250*. **Sambió**, Álfabakki 8, 101 Reykjavík, **T** 587 8900, www.sambio.is. *Map 1, F12, p249*. **Sambió**, Kringlan 4-12, 103 Reykjavík, **T** 588 0800. *Map 1, E7, p248*. **Sambió**, Smáralind shopping centre, Kópavogur, **T** 564 0000.

The Volcano Show, The Red Rock Cinema, Hellusund 6a, **T** 845 9548, vknudsen2000@yahoo.com. *Year round, with 3 showings daily Jul-Aug; 1-hr film ISK 900, 2 hrs ISK 1150, historical show ISK 300, student and child discounts. Map 2, H4, p251* Highly-rated and entertaining documentary film show about the nature of Iceland

! *The Girl in the Café,* Richard Curtis' TV play about romance and globalization on the eve of the G8 conference (2005), was set in Reykjavík, considered a mid-point between the US and Europe.

★ **Icelandic films**

Best

- *Noi Albinoi* (2003), Dagur Kari
- *Falcons* (2002), Friðrik Thór Friðriksson
- *101 Reykjavík* (2000), Baltasar Kormákur
- *The Icelandic Dream* (2000), Róbert I Douglas
- *Cold Fever* (1994), Friðrik Thór Friðriksson

and its volcanoes in particular. It's in English but if you want it translated into German, French or Dutch you can book a special screening. The films on offer cover the Heimaey and Surtsey eruptions, and Villi Knudsen's adventures which shows all the eruptions from 1947 to the present day.

Dance

Reykjavík has limited options for watching modern dance or ballet but if you do get the chance to see it, expect the unconventional. The occasional international touring company is also worth keeping an eye out for.

Iceland Dance Company, Listabraut 3, 103 Reykjavík, **T** 588 0900, www.id.is. *Map 1, F6, p248* Small company based at the Reykjavík City Theatre (see Theatre, p176), focusing exclusively on modern and contemporary dance. They work closely with other Icelandic artists and have commissioned music from everyone from rap group Quarashi to low-fi ambient group Múm.

Music

The Icelandic music scene, like much else in the country, is dominated by Reykjavík and is like nothing you've ever heard before. The one artist you will have heard of is Björk, and if she's a paradigm for what's to come, you can see why it's all so unique. She's highly regarded, drowning in awards and adulation, and often seen around the city even though she doesn't really live here any more. Rock and pop, if that's how you can classify her music, is by far the most popular form of music in the city. Don't be surprised if every second person under 30 you meet is in a band. This must be how *Gaukurinn* (officially called *Gaukur á Stöng*, see p165) can keep putting on live music every night.

The biggest new thing in recent years has been the ambient, trippy and spiritual music of Sigur Rós, a band who defy convention and description. They've had recent success putting old Icelandic tales to music and lead singer Jónsi plays his guitar with a violin bow and croons out his lyrics in a language he calls *hopelandish*, a fusion of Icelandic and English. It's hard to describe them as they're so unusual, but suffice it to say that the drummer of *Metallica* was moved to write a letter of thanks to them after hearing them. Their first album, *Ágætis Byrjun*, won numerous accolades worldwide, though their second, the obscurely-titled *( )*, received mixed reviews; they're now on their fourth album. The strangeness of some of the other ambient music on offer provides a perfect accompaniment to the weird lava formations and scenes you'll see just outside the city, with notable artists including Gús Gús, Trabant, Múm, the Leaves and Emiliana Torrini. There isn't so much in the way of rap or ethnic music, presumably because there are neither any ghettos, or much ethnic diversity.

There's only one big outdoor stadium for touring bands, the football ground at Laugardalur. Tickets for events here can be bought at either of the record shops on Laugavegur. *NASA* in Austurvöllur Square (see p165) is also big enough to host the odd band or two. Both of these venues as well as the smaller cafes and certainly *Gaukurinn* will be filled during October's Icelandic Airwaves music festival, drawing the cream of Icelandic bands as well as a few foreign imports (see Festivals, p178, for more details). In the summer the town squares are alive with free pop and rock

Pixie princess of pop

If you've heard of any famous Icelander, Björk Gudmunsdóttir is probably the one you know. Born on a commune, with an album out by the age of 11, and a member of the bands *Kukl* and *The Sugarcubes* in the 80s, Björk became an international star with the release of her first solo album, *Debut*, in 1993. Almost always described in the press as 'elfin', she quickly became known for her distinctive, beguiling voice, married with the cutting edge of electronic beats. A classically trained musician, lately her music has gone from clubby to classical, recording with the Brodsky Quartet and touring the opera houses of the world with orchestras, a choir of Inuit women from Greenland, music boxes, a harpist and even a Canadian throat-singer. Björk has said her mission is "to make modern Icelandic pop music", and describes the album *Homogenic* as "a love album to Iceland's nature", and the song *Jóga* as a kind of national anthem. Her voice and her songs capture the ethereal, heavenliness of the country as well as its earthy, sensual, throbbingly volcanic side. But she's not just known for her music. In 2000 Björk won the Palme d'Or for Best Actress at the Cannes Film Festival in 2000 for her role in *Dancer In The Dark*, Lars von Trier's tragic musical about a Czech woman slowly losing her sight. She then raised the showbiz gossip stakes when she turned up to the Oscars in a dress resembling a dead swan and proceeded to lay an egg on the red carpet. In late 2002 her mother even hit the headlines while leading a successful hunger strike against the building of a hydroelectric plant above the precious natural area of Vatnajökull glacier. Björk's latest escapades include undertaking a 10-week sailing course in order to captain a 30 tonne boat. When completed she plans to embark on an epic journey round the world with her family in 2006 .

Arts and entertainment

The sound of silence
A silent trumpeter outside Perlan celebrates the country's musical heritage.

gigs and it's worth keeping an eye out too for the art galleries as many have hosted the likes of Sigur Rós and Múm in their echoey, slightly pretentious spaces. If you're interested in music, pay a visit to the Bad Taste Gallery (see p53), the record label which launched many of Iceland's best-known bands.

Classical music and jazz is somewhat overshadowed by this, but you can still find it, often at small quirky venues like the Nordic House for occasional intimate recitals and Hallgrímskirkja for organ recitals. As you go out into the smaller villages and the countryside you could stumble upon anything from a singalong around an old piano to an accordion group.

Rock and pop

Gaukur á Stöng, Tryggvagata 22, **T** 551 1556, www.gaukurinn.is. *Map 2, D3, p250*   Also known as *Gaukurinn*, this three-floored building is the number one venue for Icelandic rock, pop and DJ sets with some form of music every night of the week. You can usually see a couple of bands for IS K 500, cheaper than the price of a cinema ticket.

Grand Rokk , Smiðjustígur 6, **T** 551 5522. *Map 2, E6, p250*   This is the best place if you want something heavy metal and gothic, with the occasional bit of rock'n'roll thrown in too.

Classical

It's possible to find classical music in other venues to the ones stated here, for example art galleries and the **Nordic House** (see p45), so keep your eyes open. Organ recitals are held in **Hallgrímskirkja** on Sunday lunchtimes and evenings during the summer, contact the tourist office for more details.

★ Icons of Icelandic culture

Best

- Érro (pop artist), p54
- Sigur Rós (post-rock band), p171
- Björk (musician), p172
- Leif Eiriksson (Viking who discovered America), p221
- Vigdís Finnbogadóttir (former Prime Minister), p224
- Halldór Laxness (novelist), p226

The Icelandic Symphony Orchestra, Háskólabíó, Hagatorg, **T** 545 2500. *Map 1, F1, p248* Prestigious orchestra playing great classical works. Tickets range from ISK 1100 to ISK 3500.

The Icelandic Opera, Ingólfsstræti, 101 Reykjavík, **T** 511 4200, www.opera.is. *Map 2, E4, p250* The opera is housed in a modern basalt building behind Ingólfshóll. There are a couple of performances a year between September and June. Tickets cost ISK 1500-5500.

Jazz

There isn't a main jazz venue in Reykjavík and you may have to hunt it out only to find a very modern version of what you're looking for. As with rock and pop, keep an eye out as things change and concerts can happen anywhere. A low-key jazz festival is held in the city at the beginning of October.

Jómfrúin, on Lækjargata. *Map 2, E3, p250* Has occasional mid-afternoon sessions in the summer.

Café Rósenberg, Lækjargata 2, **T** 551 8008. *Map 2, E3, p250* This café/bar has old instruments on the walls and often has live bands playing jazz and blues.

Theatre

If you arrive in Reykjavík in the summer the options for experiencing Icelandic theatre are limited, mainly because the National Theatre has its annual break at this time. At other times of year, drama in the city varies according to supply and demand, and the National Theatre in particular can show anything from Shakespeare and Chekhov to West End musicals and opera.

The National Theatre, Hverfisgata, 101 Reykjavík, **T** 551 1200. *Map 2, E5, p250* Box office open daily 1300-1800 except Monday, and until 2000 on days of performance. Information about the programme can be found at the tourist information centre.

The Saga of Guðridur, Skemmtihúsið, Laufasvegur 22, opposite the American Embassy, tickets available from the tourist office in Bankstræti, **T** 562 3045. *Thu-Sat at 2030 from 13 Jun-Sep. Map 2, G4, p251* A one-woman play about the journey of an Icelandic woman who toured the high seas in the 10th century and became the first European female to see North America. It's very entertaining and an interesting account of the Viking era, for tourists.

Reykjavík City Theatre, Listabraut 3, Kringlan, **T** 568 8000, www.borgarleikhus.is. *Map 1, F6, p248* The box office is open daily between 1300 and 1800 and information about the programme can also be found at the tourist information centre.

Traditional celebrations were once at the heart of the Icelandic community, providing a reason to get together and promote a feeling of nationhood against the backdrop of isolated farmsteads. Nowadays the traditional feasts, featuring marching bands and lots of dried cod, still survive alongside a host of modern festivals heralding the new identity of the country.

Perhaps the most notable of these new celebrations is the Iceland Airwaves, which showcases the country's burgeoning reputation as Europe's music capital of cool. And Iceland being Iceland, the festival calendar includes everything from the sublime to the ridiculous: from a day spent eating cream buns to what has been dubbed the best festival in the world. This latter extravaganza takes place on Heimaey in the Westman Islands on the first weekend in August, when 10,000 people come together camp, drink, party and drink some more, recovering the next day to catch baby puffins and send them out to sea until they get bigger. How refreshingly different.

January

New Year's Day (1st) A national holiday when almost everything closes and Icelanders recover from the excesses of the night before.

February

Winter Festival A three-day festival held in Reykjavík to celebrate the winter. It's also called *Festival of Light* and features a vast array of art and cultural projects around the theme of lights, to compensate for the lack of it.

Bun Day (24th) Three days of celebrations beginning with the eating of cream buns.

Bursting Day (25th) Meat dishes are eaten till people are fit to burst.

Food and Fun Festival Annual week-long food festival at the end of the month, featuring national and international chefs.

March

Spring Equinox (20th) No celebrations but it marks the moment when the hours of daylight finally equal those of darkness.

Easter Holy Thursday marks the start of the Easter holidays and a five-day weekend. Most business, banks and shops are closed.

April

Dead Week Students preparing to take their graduate exams parade around the streets dressed up in costumes.

First Day of Summer (1st Thursday after 18th) A public holiday and a time of celebrations and parades, even though it still feels like winter.

May

Labour Day (1st) A public holiday celebrated by an annual parade around the city centre.

Reykjavík Arts Festival An annual two-week festival promoting Icelandic and international culture with exhibitions, concerts, theatre, dance and opera performances.

June

Festival of the Sea (1st weekend) Annual event centring around the harbour, based on an old Icelandic tradition to honour those who make their living from the sea. There are numerous cultural activities, parades, arts and crafts activities for kids, food fairs and sailing competitions.

Icelandic National Day (17th) The day when Icelanders celebrate becoming a republic with an explosion of red, blue and white colours. When power moved from Denmark back to the country in 1944, the birth date of the leader of the independence movement Jón Sigurdsson was chosen as the day for celebration.

Summer Solstice (21st) The longest day of the year. The sun rises at 0254 and doesn't set until 2404.

The Arctic Open (26-29) Annual golf tournament held in the midnight sun at Akureyri Golf Club, a four-day international event for amateurs and professionals.

July

Landsmót Horse Show (2-7) Held in Skagafjörður in North Iceland, this is the annual horse show with parades and competitions between the various riders and breeders. Contact **T** 453 8860, landsmot@horses.is, for further information.

August

Summer Bank Holiday/Þjóðhátíð (1st weekend) Celebrating the traditional shopkeepers' break, this bank holiday, held on the first weekend in August, is celebrated with wild parties, particularly on the Westman Islands, which host the wildest Icelandic party of the year. You should book well in advance if you plan to visit. See p99, for more details.

Gay Pride (2nd weekend) Originally invented to fight for gay people's rights, this annual event draws visitors from far and wide. Thousands of people gather to march through the streets of Reykjavík. Celebrations include an outdoor concert with Icelandic and international artists, with dancing and other activities.

Reykjavík Cultural Night and Marathon (3rd weekend) Associated with the birthday of the city, all sorts of celebrations take place late into the night with music and fireworks taking centre stage. The Reykjavík marathon is held during the day with thousands of people of all ages taking part.

September

Reykjavík Film Festival Screenings of Icelandic and international films, particularly art-house movies. Runs during September and October.

Festivals and events

Reykjavík Jazz Festival National and international musicians play in venues across the capital during the early part of the month.

October

Iceland Airwaves Four days in mid-October celebrating Icelandic rock and pop music with a few international appearances amid the local talent. Venues include the Blue Lagoon. For details visit www.icelandairwaves.com.

December

Independence Day (1st) Anniversary of the day in 1918 when Iceland was granted home rule from Denmark. It's a bank holiday throughout the country.

Winter Solstice (21st) The shortest day of the year. The sun rises at 1122 and sets at 1530, barely skimming the horizon.

Þorláksmessa (23rd) This day pays tribute to St Þorlákur, one of the few indigenous saints of Iceland. Shops are open until 2300 for last-minute Christmas shopping.

Christmas Day (25th) A public holiday. Many Icelanders visit family and friends and celebrate with festive food.

New Year's Eve (31st) Icelanders say goodbye to the old year with an enormous firework displays which illuminate the sky at midnight.

Shopping

If you're a shopaholic, Reykjavík is somewhere you could go cold turkey. There are some idiosyncratic fashion and craft shops selling Icelandic specialities from knitwear to wooden bowls and jewellery, and you can get hold of some interesting Icelandic literature and music at not too eye-watering prices, but, in the main, shopping in Reykjavík cannot compete with any of Europe's capital cities. The centre is full of tourist shops selling the usual postcards and trinkets, but wander up Skólavorðustígur and browse through the craft shops for something more personal.

Shopping malls like *Smáralind* in Kópavogur and *Kringlan* have English, European and American shops, though goods are more expensive than those you'll find on Laugavegur, the main shopping street in the city. Shops are generally open Monday to Saturday 1000-1700, with the exception of the out-of-town malls and supermarkets and *Mál og Menning* bookshops, which are open later, and *Kolaportið* which is open on Sundays.

You'll find that some things are expensive, like food in general, but other things aren't so bad. Jewellery, in particular Icelandic gold and silver, is very good value and you can pick up a uniquely designed bargain here. Designer clothes are often more reasonably priced here too, especially if you claim VAT back at the airport. Icelandic wool is rightly famed for its softness and warmth, but you won't see many people wearing the traditional Icelandic jumper, the *lopapeysa* or *lopi*, except for the occasional tourist and it's a highly priced souvenir at around ISK 8000.

Skólavörðustígur, with its many boutiques and galleries, is one of the best places to start looking if you want to take home some Icelandic art or design, while Laugavegur is where you'll find *Prada* as well as many individual boutiques, plus the impressive bookshop *Mál og Menning*, which has other outlets in the city, and some craft shops. The fact that this is the main shopping street in Reykjavík isn't exactly a well-kept secret – there's even a huge sign above it telling you. It's obvious that this is the place to be because there aren't that many shops in town itself. Reykjavík is the cheapest place in Iceland to buy things as shopkeepers in smaller towns take advantage of their monopoly to hike up prices.

Off-licences are state controlled and very expensive compared with normal European prices; these shops make bringing your duty-free limit into the country worth it. An average bottle of wine costs around ISK 1300 and a four-pack of beer is about ISK 850.

Bookshops

Bókavarðan, Vesturgata 17, near the old harbour. *Map 2, C1, p250* Unusual second-hand bookshop containing more than 40,000 English and Icelandic books, 1950s pictures, magazines and much much more. The literal translation is 'book cairn' and it's a treasure trove for bibliophiles interested in the bond between literature and the Icelanders.

Sweet tooth
*Get yourself down to the sjoppa – Icelandic for shop – for some of
Iceland's most palatable delights: salt licorice, hot dogs and
retro-packaged Opal sweets.*

Mál og Menning, Laugavegur 18, **T** 552 3740, Bankastræti 2,
and Kringlan Mall, www.malogmenning.is. *Map 2, E4 and F6, p250;
Map 1, E6, p248* Exceptional Icelandic chain with a full range of
books in English and other languages on Iceland and textbooks
for learning Icelandic. The Laugavegur branch has a café upstairs
and is open until 2200. At the Bankastræti branch next to the
tourist office there's a full range of travel guides and souvenirs.
These shops also have displays of Icelandic CDs so you can pick
up the best of whatever you like while you're in town. CDs are
expensive here and not much cheaper than buying on import
in your own country.

⭐ **Best**

Icelandic CDs

- *Ágætis Byrjun* – Sigur Rós
- *Greatest Hits* – Björk
- *Moment of Truth* – Trabant
- *Life's too Good* – Sugarcubes
- *Fisherman's woman* – Emiliana Torrini
- *Summer Make Good* – Múm
- *Attention* – Gús Gús
- *Jinx* – Quarashi
- *Mugimama, Is This Monkey Music?* – Mugison

Peninn Eymundsson, Austurstræti 18, 110 Reykjavík, **T** 511 1130, www.penninn.is. *Map 2, F6, p250* Has an excellent selection of maps, magazines and souvenirs as well as a large selection of English language books.

Clothes

For boutique and designer clothing try: **Eva**, Laugavegur 91, **T** 562 0625, www.ntc.is. *Map 2, G8, p250* Part of the Northern Trading Company, a modern, fashionable boutique selling quality classics. **Flex**, Bankastræti 11, **T** 551 3930. *Map 2, E4, p250* A Saevar Karl boutique with an interior design to match. There's even an art gallery on the premises.

Illgresi, off Laugavegur, in a small alley opposite *Mál og Menning* bookshop. *Map 2, F6, p250* Funky second-hand clothing shop. Also here is **Plastikk**, a kitsch boutique.

Sputnik, Laugavegi 51, 101 Reykjavík, **T** 561-7060, *Map 2, F8, p250* Where the funky boho Reykjavíkurs get their indie kid look. **Prada**, Bankastræti, opposite Þingholtsstræti. *Map 2, E4, p250*

Shopping

Spaks Manns Spjarir, Bankastræti 11, **T** 551 2090. *Map 2, E4, p250* Unusual Icelandic fashion design that fits in nicely with the surroundings here, though whether or not it will suit the suburbs back home is another matter.

Craft and design

Kirsuberjatréð, Vesturgata 4, **T**562 8990, www.kirs.is. *Map 2, C1, p250* For something truly unique. It sells individually designed jewellery, fish-skin products – more beautiful than they sound - and Icelandic wool-covered energy stones.

Jewellery

Specialist jewellers and watchmakers include: **Franch Michelson**, Laugavegur 15, **T** 511 1900; **Fridða Thomas**, Bröttugötu 3a, **T** 867 8451, www.fridathomas.com; **Gull & Silfur,** Laugavegi 52, **T** 552 0620; **Gullkúnst**, Laugavegi 45, **T** 561 6660; **Jens**, Kringlan, 103 Reykjavík, **T** 568 6730; **Hermann Jónsson**, Vultusund 3, 101 Reykjavík, **T** 551 3014; and **Lára Gullsmður**, Skólavörðustig 10, **T** 561 1300.

Markets

Kolaportið, Geirsgata, **T** 562 5030. *Sat-Sun 1100-1700. Map 2, C3/D3, p250* In Kolaportið flea market you'll find a host of bric-a-brac stalls, second-hand clothing and a wide range of Icelandic books. One look at the stalls and you won't be surprised to find that the Icelanders publish more books per head than any other nation. There are also a few souvenir and craft stalls that are markedly less expensive and more interesting than the shops in town.

Towards the back of the hall is the main event – the fish market. You can try the famous *hákarl* as well as dried fish, huge fresh fulmar eggs and a lot of fish cheaper than at the supermarket. Unlike the majority of places in Reykjavík, you'll need cash to buy from the stalls, but there's a handy ATM by the toilets near the east entrance.

Off-licences

Vinbúðin Austurstræti, next door to *Planet City* on Austurstræti, **T** 562 6511. *Mon-Thu 1100-1800, Fri 1100-1900, Sat 1100-1400. Map 2, D1, p250*

Vinbúðin Kringlunni , at Kringlan Mall, **T**568 9060. *Mon-Thu 1100-1800, Fri 1100-1900, Sat 1100-1600. Map 1, E6, p248*

Outdoor gear

66° North, Lækjargata 4, **T** 561 6800, is Iceland's outdoor equipment and clothing company, with a number of branches in Reykjavík. For more technical camping, climbing, hiking, cycling and fishing equipment, try **Nanoq**, Kringlan Mall, **T** 575 5100; and **Útlif**, **T** 545 1500, www.utilif.is, at both Kringlan and Smáralind shopping malls.

Shopping malls

Kringlan Mall, 112-150 Kringlumýrarbraut, 105 Reykjavík, **T** 568 9200, www.kringlan.is *Mon-Wed 1000-1830, Thu 1000-2100, Fri 1000-1900, Sat 1000-1800, Sun 1300-1700. Bus Nos 3, 5, 6, 110, 111, 112, 115, 140. Map 1, E7, p248* On the outskirts of Reykjavík, about a half-hour walk from 101 toward Perlan, is Kringlan Mall. It's got a very different atmosphere from the shopping street in downtown Reykjavík with a number of chain fashion and homeware stores from Europe. It also has an off-licence, or *vínbúðin*. There's also a bookshop and a post office and the third floor is home to a load of fast-food outlets, mainly American, and the toilets. The cinema and restaurants are open later in the evening and at weekends.

Smáralind Mall, Hagasmáril, 201 Kópavogur, www.smarlaind.is. *Mon-Fri 1100-1900, Sat 1100-1800, Sun 1300-1800. Bus Nos 16, 17, 18, 114.* The newer of the two malls, further from the city centre but with less idiosyncratic Icelandic offerings. There are 70 stores including *Gap*, *Debenhams*, *Jack & Jones*, *Nokia*, *Zara*, *Mango*, *Benetton* and occasional photographic exhibitions on the ground floor. The food hall includes *TGI Friday*, *Pizza Hut* and the ubiquitous hot dogs. There's also a crèche and a cinema complex.

Supermarkets

There are a number of supermarkets in the centre of Reykjavík if you're self-catering. Try **10-11** on Austurstræti, *Map 2, D3, p250*, **Bónus**, on Laugavegur, *Map 2, F8, p250* and **Hagkaup**, which is a lot larger, at Kringlan Mall (see above).

Because Reykjavík is both Iceland's capital and marooned in a wild open space, there are a huge number of sporting activities available here from the more refined ice-skating, badminton and spectator sports to activities on glaciers, under lava and on horseback.

One thing that you shouldn't miss while you're in Iceland is the swimming. There are seven pools in Reykjavík alone, all geothermally heated, not counting a beach, the Blue Lagoon and a hot mountain spring in the central highlands, at Landmannalaugar.

Both Lara Croft and James Bond have been seen romping around out here, in *Tomb Raider* and *Die Another Day* respectively, enough to prove that skidooing and dog sledding aren't going out of fashion. Many of the tour operators offer day trips to glaciers including these activities and you should only attempt them with a guide, for obvious reasons. Fishing and riding equipment brought into the country must be fully disinfected and carry a vet's certificate.

Fishing

Iceland's lakes and rivers are populated with trout and salmon. The fishing season runs from April to September and you need a permit to fish in most rivers. Salmon fishing needs to be booked long in advance but trout-fishing permits are available at short notice. Prices are dependent on where you're fishing, the yield and the time of year. Trout fishing costs around ISK 1000 per day depending on the season and equipment can be hired from fishing shops. Ice fishing is also possible in winter on Lake Reynisvatn, 15 minutes from Reykjavík.

Reykjavík Angling Club, Háaleitisbraut 68, 103 Reykjavík, **T** 568 6050, www.svfr.is. The central angling club and offers Permits, advice and maps of the best fishing areas.

Veiðihornið, Hafnarstræti 5, **T** 551 6760, www.veidihornid.is. The main fishing shop in Reykjavík selling permits and offering advice about freshwater fishing.

Football

Football is Iceland's main sport, along with handball. The women's football team have been particularly successful in Europe and the men's narrowly missed out on qualifying for the recent World Cup. It has been cruelly said that the national team has the same amount of success you'd expect of a team from a small town playing teams from countries ten times the size, and it is something of a marvel that Iceland has managed to produce a couple of footballers who play in Europe. Internationals and some local matches are held at the sports stadium in Laugardalur; contact the tourist office for further information. The official site of the Football Association in Iceland is www.ksi.is.

Glacier hiking

Icelandic Mountain Guides, Vagnhofdi 7b, 110 Reykjavík, **T** 587 9999, www.mountainguide.is. Runs summer tours around Skaftafell National Park in the north and tours from Reykjavík to Sólheimajökull glacier, Hengill geothermal area and Heiðmörk Nature Reserve. They also run climbing, backpacking and polar expeditions on request. For the Laugavegurinn walk from Landmannalaugar, see p98.

Iceland Touring Association, **T** 568 2533, www.fi.is. As well as offering advice, the ITA operates a number of mountain huts where hikers can stay in sleeping-bag accommodation (book in advance). It also offers a variety of tours including hiking and cross country skiing.

Golf

Akureyri Golf Club, **T** 462 2974, 1 km north of Akureyri on the north coast. The most northerly 18 hole golf course in the world is host to the Arctic Open, which is played in mid-June under the midnight sun. Extensive clubhouse facilities include changing rooms, restaurant, bar and pro-shop. Hire facilities available.

Golfklúbbur Vestmannaeyjar, PO Box 168, 902 Vestmannaeyjar, **T** 481 2363, www.eyjar.is/golf. The Vestmannaeyjar Golf Course is among one of the most unusual in the world with a yearly Volcanic Open, several patches of rough lava and a view of the sea. You can play in the midnight sun in summer – just watch out for the puffins!

Golf Federation of Iceland, Engjavegi 6, **T** 514 4050, www.golf.is. Useful for information about events.

★ Horse riding

A trek on an Icelandic horse is a highly recommended way to see the Icelandic countryside and a relaxing wallow in a hot tub when you come back is the best way to soothe your aching muscles. There are a number of stables offering day and half-day tours just outside Reykjavík. The closest is *Ís Hestar*, and for the others you can be picked up in town. If you're an experienced rider you can also join longer tours across the interior of the county rounding up the sheep and seeing the natural wonders, again with *Ís Hestar*.

You can also go pony trekking on Heimaey, in the Westmann Islands (see p99), around the lava, up to see the puffins or whatever you fancy doing. An hour costs around ISK 2000 and you have free rein on where you want to go, **T** 481 1478.

Eldhestar, Vellir, 810 Hveragerdi, **T** 480 4800, www.eldhestar.is. Stables in Hveragerdi, about 40 minutes from the city, offering day tours in the lava, around Hekla and other hot springs including the Blue Lagoon. A 1-2 hour tour costs from ISK 2800 and day tours are from ISK 8900, pick-up at city hotels and guesthouses included.

Ís Hestar, Sörlaskeið 26, 220 Hafnarfjörður, **T** 555 7000, www.ishestar.is. Offers a wide range of half-day tours from the mystical lava fields around Hafnarfjörður where you might see the odd elf or two. Longer tours also available and a connection with *Iceland Excursions* (see p29) means you can ride in the morning and visit the Golden Circle or Blue Lagoon in the afternoon. Prices start at ISK 4600 for a lava tour. The lava tour plus Blue Lagoon trip costs ISK 7700, lunch and pick-up at hotels and guesthouses included.

! In 1972 the World Chess Championships were held in Iceland. When American genius Bobby Fischer beat Russian Boris Spassky it was hailed as a Cold War victory.

Sports

Íslenskir Ferðahestar, Víðigrund, Mosfellsbær, **T** 894 7200, www.centrum.is/travelhorse. Tours of Þingvellir during the day and at midnight and also the historical Mosfellsdalur valley where Halldór Laxness lived. Prices from ISK 3900 for two hours to 7500 for a seven-hour excursion.

Laxnes Horse Farm, 270 Mosfellsbær, **T** 566 6179, www.laxnes.is. Also in literary Mosfellsbær, the former home of Halldór Laxness and the final resting place of Égil Skallagrímsson of *Égil's Saga*, *Laxnes* offers three-hour tours for ISK 3500 and seven-hour tours including lunch and coffee for ISK 8000 as well as trips to Þingvellir. There's also a discount for families and 15% off for students.

Þyrill Horse Trekking, **T** 588 7887, www.thyrill.is. Organizes treks through the volcanic craters of Rauðhólar, the Blue Lagoon and Lake Elliðavatn just outside the city. Pick-ups for riders at 0930 and 1330 daily from their hotels. Light lunch included. Trips cost ISK 3500-7000 including pick-up.

Pólar Hestar, Grýtubakki II, 601 Akureyri, **T** 463 3179, www.nett.is/polar. Day tours and longer themed treks searching for trolls, Vikings and sheep. Day tours including 6-7 hours riding, a guide and snacks costs ISK 7000. Pick-up from Akureyri is an additional ISK 1500.

Sport Tours, Kaupangur, **T** 894 2967, www.sporttours.is. Five minutes from Akureyri. Tours for one, two and three hours costing from ISK 2800.

! Cairns at the side of the less well-used roads mark old walking trails as well as the edge of the road in bad weather. Some have been used to create the GPS network in Iceland, the modern way of finding your route in bad weather.

Sports

> ## Horse play
>
> When the Vikings came to Iceland in the year 874 they brought Norwegian horses with them and no horse has been imported into the country since. The two most striking things about the horses are their friendly temperament and unusual gait. Most horses have the three basic gaits, but the Icelandic horse has the full range of walk, trot, canter, *tölt* and pace or *flying* pace. The *tölt* is only found in a few horse breeds across the world, a way of running where the horse only has one foot on the ground at any one time. It's such a smooth ride that the rider can carry a glass of wine and not spill a drop. Well, when it's this expensive you wouldn't want to. The pace is unique to this breed. They run like a camel, with both feet on one side lifted from the ground alternately which is a slightly gawky look, but impressive nonetheless.

Skidoos and husky dogs

Dog-sledding is seasonal and takes place from January to August, depending on the snow. Skidoo trips can take place all year round.

Dog Steam Tours, Bolholt, 851 Hella, **T** 487 7747, www.dog sledding.is. Runs glacier tours in winter and summer with beautiful blue-eyed Greenland husky dogs or skidoos. One-hour tours in South Iceland on either Vatnajökull, Mýrðalsjökull or Langjökull cost ISK 6500, two-hour dog training trips when there isn't any snow cost the same. Pick-up from Reykjavík is also available.

Eskimos, Tunguháls 19, 110 Reykjavík, **T** 414 1500, www.eskimos.is. Runs organized and customized tours to glaciers including snow-mobiling and dog-sledding. An eight-hour tour to Langjökull glacier costs from ISK 23,500 or from ISK 19,500 on the highlands.

Swimming

Swimming in Reykjavík is an unmissable activity, whether you go to the Blue Lagoon (see p80) or find the time to relax in a family-orientated local pool. Unlike other spa towns across the world, the majority of the pools are outdoor municipal pools or lidos with the added bonus of hot pots and steam rooms. Swimming is the national sport and all Icelanders have to be able to swim before they can graduate from school. Families use the hot pools and thermal spas to relax and chat in as primarily a social occasion especially early in the morning and after work.

More natural outdoor swimming areas can be found at Landmannalaugar, about a four-hour drive from the city where the hot springs mix with the natural stream. You can even swim in the heated water of the beach beneath the Pearl at Nauthólsvík (see p65). All the swimming pools listed below are in Reykjavík, unless stated otherwise, and cost ISK 250, ISK 110 for children.

Árbæjarlaug, Fylkisvegur, **T** 510 7600. *Mon-Fri 0630-2230, Sat-Sun 0800-2030, till 2300 in summer. Bus 10, 11, 110.* Great for families, this outdoor pool has a wonderful view of the countryside as well as hot tubs and a steam room. Highly recommended.

Breiðholtslaug, Austurberg, **T** 557 5547. *Mon-Fri 0630-2200, Sat-Sun 0800-2000. Bus 14, 12, 112.* Particularly good if you're swimming for exercise rather than to socialize.

Grafarvogslaug, Dalhús, **T** 510 4600. *Mon-Fri 0630-2230, Sat-Sun 0800-2030. Bus 14 or 15* Large swimming pool that's part of a new sports complex with indoor and outdoor pools, hot pots and jacuzzi.

Kjalarneslaug, Kléberg, **T** 566 6879. *Mon-Fri 1700-2100, Sat-Sun 1100-1700. Bus 20.* Friendly pool on the outskirts of Reykjavík with a small outdoor pool, hot pots and sauna.

> ### Swimming pool etiquette

Because the water is mainly untreated, there is an etiquette that you must follow in the thermal pools. First take off your shoes outside the changing area. Then strip off completely and take a shower. There's soap/shampoo on the walls of the showers and it's expected that you will wash completely before going into the pool. Then put on your swimming costume and head for the water. There have been occasions where visitors have been told to go back and wash, so do as the locals do and you'll be okay. Hot pots are marked with the temperature on the outside in Celsius so you can make an educated guess rather than plunging into something more suitable for a lobster and making an embarrassing exit.

Laugardalslaug Thermal Pool, Laugardalur, **T** 553 4039. *Mon- Fri 0630-2230, Sat-Sun 0800-2030, till 2300 in summer. Bus 5*. The biggest of the city's seven outdoor pool, attracting tourists and residents alike for the 50 m pool, slide, hot pots, steam room and sauna.

Sundhöllin, Barónsstígur, **T** 551 4059. *Mon-Fri 0630-2200, Sat-Sun 0800-1900*. The only indoor swimming pool with hot tubs outside and a steam room. Not so exciting for children, but good if you just want to swim.

Vesturbæjarlaug, Hofsvallagata, **T** 551 5004. *Mon-Fri 0630-2200, Sat-Sun 0800-2000*. Pleasant outdoor pool with hot pots and a large glass-walled steam room.

Akureyri Swimming Pool, Þingvallastræti 21, 600 Akureyri, **T** 461 4455. *ISK 270, ISK 140 children 6-15*. Good for all ages with hot tubs, outdoor pool, water slide, solarium and steambath. This is the best of the two swimming pools and a great way to ease tired, aching feet.

Icelandic pastimes

Best

- Ignoring celebrities
- Overusing superlatives
- Admiring forests
- Drinking very strong coffee
- Talking about the weather

On **Heimaey** there's an indoor geothermal pool with hot pots and a big pool, **T** 481 1149. *Mon-Fri 0700-2100, Sat-Sun 0900-1700 in summer. ISK 200.*

Whitewater rafting and kayaking

Rivers accessible from Reykjavík for whitewater rafting are mainly a drive away in the south of Iceland where there are a number of different levels at which to raft. The north of Iceland has some of the best rivers for rafting. Varmahlíð can easily be reached from Akureyri by bus or car. Most of the activity based tour operators can organize rafting and kayking.

Activity Tours, 560 Varmahlíð, **T** 453 8383, www.rafting.is. Various tours for differing abilities in the north, specializing in rafting but also offering kayaking, fishing, horse riding and other activities.

Arctic rafting, Lækjarsel 9, 109 Reykjavík **T** 898 0410, www.arctic rafting.is. Trips for beginners and the more experienced down the Þjórsá, Markarfljót and Hólmsá rivers. The trips leave from Selfoss in the south costing ISK 5900-6900, minimum six people.

Sport Tours, Hafnarstræti 82, 600 Akureyri, **T** 461 2968, www.sporttours.is. River rafting plus pick-up in Akureyri from ISK 6500. Again in the north.

Gay and lesbian

Reykjavík is a very open place and is welcoming towards members of the gay community. Bars and clubs are open to all-comers and it's unlikely that you'll encounter any problems in the city. Icelanders are very forward-looking and welcoming to all, especially in Reykjavík. Should you encounter any difficulties or problems in the city, the Gay and Lesbian Community Centre is very friendly and helpful in all areas and tourists and locals alike are welcome to join them in their bar. Apart from the *MSC* bar, the bars listed are mixed venues that have proved particularly popular with the gay scene. The annual Gay Pride parade on the second weekend in August has been celebrated for the last three years and is steadily growing in popularity (see Festivals, p178). The websites www.gayice.is and www.gay.mis.is are useful for listings and information.

Sleeping

The House of the Spirits, Gardastraeti 8, 101 Reykjavík, **T** 698 3526, www.geocities.com/houseofspirits101. *Map 2, E1, p250* A charming house with fully equipped kitchen. Gay owned and run.

Room with a view Laugavegur 18, **T** 896 2559, www.room withaview.is. *Map 2, F6, p250 See also p122* Gay-owned flats above *Mál og Menning*.

Tower Guesthouse, Grettisgata 6, **T** 896 6694, www.tower.is. *Map 2, G8, p251 See also p122* Luxurious central guesthouse and apartments with elegant rooms, kitchens and bathrooms in a refined and courtly atmosphere. Balcony overlooking the bay with jacuzzi.

Eating and drinking

Café Opera, Lækjargata 2, **T** 552 9499, www.cafeopera.is. *Daily 1800-0100, Fri-Sat 1800-0300, kitchen open to 2330, 0100 Fri-Sat. Map 2, E3, p250 See also p142* Opera, as it's known to locals, is a traditional restaurant with a cosy antique atmosphere and an choice of food and wine. There's a cosy wine bar upstairs.

Jómfrúin, Lækjargata 4, 101 Reykjavík, **T**551 0100. *1100-2200 in summer, till 1900 in winter. Map 2, E3, p250 See also p148* Danish open sandwiches served in this restaurant in the heart of town. It's especially good for brunch on a Saturday afternoon in the summertime.

Gay and lesbian

Bars and clubs

Bar 22, Laugavegur 22, 101 Reykjavík. *Map 2, F6, p250 See also p160* Playing pop and indie music, *Bar 22* is a hip bar in the centre of town with reasonably priced food and bar snacks, and dancing and drinking until late. Open to all, but particularly popular with the gay scene. No entry fee.

Café Cozy, Austurstræti 3, 101 Reykjavík. Sun-Thu 1000-0100, Fri-Sat 0800-0600. *Map 2, D2, p250* The main gay bar in Iceland. It's a friendly café with a relaxed atmosphere. A good place for an English breakfast, lunch or to mingle in the evening.

MSC Iceland, Bankastræti 11, 101 Reykjavík, **T** 562 1280, www.msc.is. *Sat from 2300. Map 2, E5, p250* Opposite the opera, this is a men-only leather club similar to others throughout Europe. Visitors are welcome.

Sirkus, Klapparstígur 31, 101 Reykjavík. *Map 2, E6, p250 See also p166* A little like a beach hut from the outside, *Sirkus* is a hip hang-out with palm trees painted on the wall, a kitsch interior and laid-back retro indie and hip-hop music. Popular with the arts, music and gay scene, expect the unexpected from topless lesbian dancing to more general madness. No entry fee, live music/DJs three times a week, beer ISK 550.

Organizations

Gay and Lesbian community centre (Samtokin 78),
Laugavegur 3, 4th floor, **T** 552 7878, www.samtokin78.is. *Mon-Thu 2000-1130, Sat from 2100. Map 2, E5, p250* The centre is a relaxed place to meet, with a bar, library and media suite, and is welcoming to both locals and tourists alike.

One of the most noticeable things about Reykjavík is how happy the children are, and how many of them there are. Kids here are gregarious, friendly and welcomed virtually everywhere. There isn't a huge divide between children and adults – children are included in mainstream society as a rule – and people have children at a younger age than in much of Europe. It's also so safe in the city that children often play unminded on the streets.

Laugardalur Valley has a wide range of activities suitable for children and many day-tour operators offer free tours or considerable discounts for under-12s. Swimming pools are particularly suited to children, including the Blue Lagoon. Look out too for funfairs along by the old harbour where candyfloss, dried cod and carousels are the norm. Children are welcome in most restaurants in the city.

Sights

Reykjavík Park and Zoo, Hafrafell v/ Engjaveg, 105 Reykjavík,
T 575 7800, www.husdyragardur.is. *Daily 15 May-25 Aug
1000-1800, 26 Aug-14 May 1000-1700.12 years and over ISK 450, 5-12
years ISK 350, under 4s free. Bus 2, 10, 11, 12 or 15 from Lækjartorg
Sq. Map 3, E9, p253 See also p63* Behind the sports complex and
next to the Botanical Gardens, the park and zoo is only really
exciting if you're under 12. The zoo contains farm animals, reindeer
and mink and the park has a playground and boat rides on a pond.
Recent additions include an aquarium, focusing on species from
the North Atlantic, and Science World, where you can try various
hands-on exhibits like measure how loud you scream or blow huge
soap bubbles. There's a restaurant on site.

Reykjavík Botanical Garden, Skúlatún 2, 105 Reykjavík,
T 553 8870, botgard@rvk.is. *Daily Apr-Sep 1000-2200, Oct-Mar
1000-1700. Free. Bus 2, 10, 11, 12, 15. Map 3, E10, p253 See also
p63* The botanical garden is a joy on a clear sunny day, with 2½
hectares of good walking and cycling trails along the rock gardens,
Japanese-style bridges and Icelandic flora, such as it is. No dogs are
allowed and it's a good place for children with bushes to hide in, a
couple of climbing frames and a lot of open space.

Árbæjarsafn (Reykjavík City Museum), Kistuhyl 4,
110 Reykjavík, **T** 577 1111, www.arbaejarsafn.is. *Jun-Aug
Tue-Fri 0900-1700, closed Mon, Sat, Sun. Sep-May Mon, Wed, Fri
1300-1400. Map 1, D12, p249 See also p70* Open-air museum on
the outskirts of the city particularly suitable for children. There's a

! If you're having difficulties with your children, you should
read *Egil's Saga*. Egil was a problem child who at the age of six
killed another boy who was better than him at football. Puts
things in perspective a bit…

Kids

★ **Ways to keep the kids amused**

Best

- Look for whales, p33
- Feed the ducks at the Tjörnin, p42
- Check out seals and reindeer in the children's zoo, p63
- Splash about in the Blue Lagoon, p80
- Watch the spouting geysers, p87

field with sheep and Icelandic ponies, a display of life as an Icelandic child through the ages, complete with old toys, and occasional hands on demonstrations of life in rural Iceland, for example demonstrating hay threshing and other techniques. During the summer occasional shows stop off here to entertain school children. Visit the tourist office for further information about events.

Tjörnin *Map 1, E2, p248 See also p42* Just outside the City Hall is a popular area for feeding the ducks and greylag geese; at the opposite end of the pond you'll find a small children's play area with a climbing frame for monkeying around on.

Öskjuhlíð Hill *Map 1, F5/G5, p248 See also p64* The woodland area at Öskjuhlíð Hill is a good place for a walk or a bike ride, with lots of free-roaming rabbits, and just beside the Pearl building there is a man-made geyser which spouts every few minutes. Nauthólsvík Beach at the foot of the hill is also a delight for children and adults alike, with two hot pots popular with local children.

Kids

Sleeping

Family rooms are available at most youth hostels (www.hostel.is) and **Farm Holidays** (www.farmholidays.is) rent cottages by the week on a B&B basis, often including activities like riding, fishing and swimming. Those listed here are all outside Reykjavík.

B Fosshotel Husavík, Ketilsbraut 22, 640 Husavík, **T** 464 1220, www.fosshotel.is. Small professional hotel in the centre of town with all mod cons and a beautiful view of the fjord. There's also a bar and restaurant and breakfast is included.

D Árból guesthouse, Ásgarðsvegur 2, 640 Húsavík, **T** 464 2229, www.simnet.is/arbol. Comfortable small guesthouse by a stream in a corner of the village. The house dates from 1903 and is warm, romantic and homely.

D Eldá Tourist Centre Campsite and Hotel, Reynihlíð, 660 Mývatn, **T** 464 4220, www.elda.is. Small relaxed hotel and small campsite by the lake. Bring some insect repellent! B&B in the area can also be arranged as can most of the activities in the area including boating and cycling. Camping costs ISK 500 per person.

E Guesthouse Brekka, The Brekka Restaurant, 630 Hrísey, **T** 466 1751, brekkahrisey@isl.is. Small restaurant offering standard B&B accommodation in twin rooms with made-up beds or sleeping-bag accommodation. Affords impressive views of the midnight sun.

E-F Guesthouse Gullsól, Sólberg, 611 Grímsey, **T** 467 3114, grimsey@ismennt.is. Small three-roomed guesthouse with friendly personal service.

F Guesthouse Básar, 611 Grímsey, **T** 467 3103, sigrun@konica.is. The largest of the two establishments, a warm family guesthouse in Grímsey offering sleeping-bag accommodation from ISK 1700 and made-up beds.

G Hrísey Campsite, **T** 466 3012. Basic campsite perfect for getting back to nature, no mod cons. They can also arrange sleeping-bag accommodation in the local school in the summer.

Kids

Eating and drinking

Pizza 67 (see also p152) or **First Vegetarian** (see also p146) are places to try for difficult eaters. They all serve food like pizza, burgers and lasagne in less formal settings.

Sports

Bowling Keiluhöllin, Öskjuhlíð , 101 Reykjavík, **T** 511 5300, www.keiluhollin.is. *Sun-Tue 1200-2400, Fri-Sat 1200-0200.* An 18-lane bowling hall on the road leading to Öskjuhlíð Hill and a good place to keep out of the rain. Open very late on a Friday and Saturday night too, if that's your thing. Games cost from ISK 450 for children under 12 on weekdays. At weekends one game is ISK 550.

Reykjavík's many swimming pools are always full of young families and all pools except Sundhöllin have slides and basketball hoops as well as the usual hot pots. Admission for children aged 6-16 is ISK 100, free for those under six. See Swimming, p198.

Facilities and services

Reykjavík Pre-School Service, **T** 411 7000, www.leiksdar.is. If you need a bit of a break, Reykjavík council have outdoor facilities and playgrounds where you can leave your children. It costs ISK 100 for supervised play for children aged 2-6 at various playgrounds around the city, including one at Frejugata in the centre. They are primarily used by Icelanders, so it's a good idea to contact them beforehand if you're planning to use them.

! The Icelandic saying "to take someone on the bone" means to tell someone how bad they've been. This comes from an old tradition where children being told off for being naughty in school had to sit on a whale vertebra.

Directory

Airline offices
Icelandair for international flights, Keflavík Airport, **T** 505 0300, www.icelandair.com. **Air Iceland** for internal flights, Reykjavík Airport, **T** 570 3030.

Banks and ATMs
Banks are open Mon-Fri 0915-1600. All banks change foreign currency and ATMs (cashpoints) are open all night long. A branch at Keflavík Airport is open 24 hrs.

Bicycle hire
Bikes can be hired from a number of places in Reykjavík for around ISK 1700 per day or ISK 1500 per half day, with discounts for longer hire. **Borgarhjól Bike Rental**, Hverfisgata 50, **T** 551 5653, is the largest bike hire company. Bikes can also be hired at the campsite at Laugardalur, 105 Reykjavík, **T** 567 6944.

Car hire
ALP Car Rental, Vatnsmýrarvegi 10, 101 Reykjavík, **T** 562 6060, www.alp.is. **ÁTAK Car Rental**, Smiðjuvegur 1, 200 Kópavogur, **T** 554 6040, www.atak.is. **Atlantis Car Rental**, Grensásvegur 14 108 Reykjavík, **T** 588 0000, www.atlantisiceland.com. **Atlas Car Rental**, Dalshrauni 9, 220 Hafnarfjörður, **T** 565 3800, www.atlas car.is. **Avis**, Duguvogur 10, 104 Reykjavík, **T** 553 1090, www.avis.is; also at Akureyri Airport and Draupnisgata 4, Akureyri, **T** 461 2428. **Berg**, Bíldshöfði 10, 112 Reykjavík, **T** 577 6050, www.carrental-berg.com. **Budget Car Rental**, Duguvogi 10, 104 Reykjavík, **T** 562 6060, www.budget.is. **Butterfly Car Rental**, Ranargata 8a, 101 Reykjavík, **T** 894 1864, www.kvasir.is/butterfly/car-rental.php. **Europcar**, Flatahraun 31, 220 Hafnarfjörður, **T** 565 3800, www.euro pcar.is. **Hertz**, Reykjavík Airport, Flugvallabraut, **T** 505 0500, www.hertz.is; Keflavík Airport, **T** 425 0221; Vestmannaeyjar Airport, **T** 481 3300; Akureyri Airport, **T** 481 3300. **National Car Rental**, Tryggvabraut 12, 600 Akureyri, **T** 461 6000, www.nationalcar.is.

Cultural institutions
Alþjóðahús (the Intercultural Centre), Hverfisgata 18, 101 Reykjavík, **T** 530 9300, www.ahus.is. Cultural centre primarily for recent immigrants offering cultural advice, legal representation and interpreters. In addition, the following centres also exist: **Alliance Française**, Hringbraut 121, **T** 530 9300, http://af.ismennt.is. **Goethe-Zentrum**, Laugavegur 18, **T** 551 6061, www.goethe.is. **Norræna Húsið**, Nordic House, corner Sæmundagata and Hringbraut, T 551 7031, www.nordice.is.

Dentists
Saturday and Sunday emergency clinic in central Reykjavík, **T** 575 0505.

Disabled
The City of Reykjavík has produced a brochure called *Accessible Reykjavík*, available at the tourist information centre, detailing accessibility of attractions, bars and restaurants in the city as well as some useful paths.

Doctors
For an ambulance call the emergency jumber **T** 112. For less serious medical emergencies, go to the emergency room ('*Slysadeild*') at the **National University Hospital**, Fossvogur, **T** 543 2000. **Medical Centre**, Smáratorg 1, Kópavogur. *Mon-Fri 1700-2300, reception 1700-0800.* Home visits and telephone consultations 24 hrs, also on public holidays. GP consultation has a flat rate of ISK 400 for adults, ISK 200 for children; house calls cost ISK 1600.

Electricity
220 volts, 50 Hz AC. Appliances use a standard European two-pin plug. Adapters are available from the tourist office.

Embassies in Iceland

Canada, Túngata 14, 101 Reykjavík, **T** 575 6500, rkjvk@inter
national.gc.ca. **Denmark**, Hverfisgata 29, 101 Reykjavík, **T** 575 0300,
rekamb@um.dk. *Mon-Fri 0900-1200*. **Finland**, Túngata 30, 101
Reykjavík, **T** 510 0100, finamb@finland.is. *Mon-Fri 0900-1200*.
France, Túngata 22, 101 Reykjavík, **T** 551 7621. *Mon-Fri 0900-1230,
1330-1700*. **Germany**, Laufásvegur 31, 101 Reykjavík, **T** 530 1100,
embager@internet.is. *Mon-Fri 0900-1200*. **Japan**, Laugavegur 182,
6th floor, 105 Reykjavík, **T** 510 8600, japan@itn.is. **Norway**,
Fjólugata 17, 101 Reykjavík, **T** 520 0700. *Mon-Fri 0900-1600*.
Sweden, Lágmúli 7, 108 Reykjavík, **T** 520 1230, sveamb@itn.is.
Mon-Fri 0900-1200. **UK**, Laufásvegur 31, 101 Reykjavík, **T** 550 5100,
britem@centrum.is. *Mon-Fri 0830-1200*. **USA**, Laufásvegur 21, 101
Reykjavík, **T** 562 9100, consularreykja@ state.gov. **Ministry of
Foreign Affairs** (all other enquiries), Rauðarárstígur 25, **T** 560 9900.

Emergency numbers

For fire, ambulance and police, **T** 112.

Hospitals

There is a 24-hr casualty department at the **Kópavogur
Fossvogur Hospital**, 108 Reykjavík, **T** 525 1700. Buses 6, 7, 14,
110, 111, 112, 115. Also at the **National University Hospital**,
Fossvogur, **T** 543 2000. There are doctors on duty 24 hrs at the **City
Hospital**, Hringbraut, 105 Reykjavík, **T** 543 1000. Buses 3, 5, 6 and 7.
The standard charge is ISK 3170.

Internet/email

There are plenty of email cafés throughout Iceland, generally
costing ISK 500 per hour. The tourist offices and libraries offer
internet access for around ISK 200 per 30 minutes. In Reykjavík you
can find free internet at **This is Iceland** information centre on
Laugavegur (see p35) and at the **Ráðhúskaffi** in the city hall (see
p151), if you buy a drink.

Language schools
The University of Iceland, Suðurgata, 101 Reykjavík, **T** 525 4593, www.hi.is. Runs a summer school in Jun as well as undergraduate and graduate courses. **Námsflokkar Reykjavíkur**, Fríkirkjuvegur1, 101 Reykjavík, **T** 551 2992, www.namsflokkar.is. Shorter courses primarily for new residents. Month-long courses are free for children and teenagers and cost ISK 5000-6500 for adults.

Launderette
There isn't a self-service laundrette as such in Reykjavík, but you can use the machines at both the campsite and the youth hostel in Laugardalur, costing around ISK 300-400 per load, see Sleeping section (p125) further details. The full-service laundrette is on Barónsstígur costing ISK 900 per load, ISK 1700 with drying and folding. Open 0800-1800 Mon-Fri, closed at weekends.

Left luggage
BSÍ bus terminal, Vatnsmýrarvegur 10, **T** 591 1000. Open daily 0730-2200, ISK 1000 per week.

Libraries
The City Library, Tryggvagata 15, 101 Reykjavík, **T** 563 1750, www.borgarbokasafn.is. *Year round, Mon-Thu 1000-2000, Fri 1100-1900, Sat-Sun 1300-1700.* **The National and University Library of Iceland**, Arngrímsgata 3, 107 Reykjavík, **T** 525 5600, www.bok.hi.is. *Jun-14 Aug Mon-Fri 0900-1700, Sat 1000-1400, closed Sun. Open 15 Aug- May Mon-Thu 0815-2200, Fri 0815-1900, Sat 0900-1700, Sun 1100-1700.*

Lost property
The main office for lost and found articles is at the police station at Borgartún 33, **T** 569 9018. *Mon-Fri 1000-1200 and 1400-1600.*

Media
Iceland Review is a glossy quarterly magazine promoting the country in English, www.icenews.is. TV news in English is avaiable on **Channel 1** and radio news on **FM 92.4/93.5** daily at 0730. **BBC World Service FM 90.9**. Also operates a telephone recording of the news which can be heard by calling **T** 515 3690. The main daily newspapers are **Morgunblaðið** and **DV**, both in Icelandic.

Pharmacies (late night)
Pharmacies are generally open 0900-1800. The following are open later. **Háaleitis Apótek**, Háaleitisbraut 68, **T** 581 2101. *Until 0200*. **Lyfja Apótek**, Lágmúli 5, Closest to the campsite in Laugardalur, **T** 533 2300. *0800-2400*. **Lyfja Apótek**, Laugarvegi 16, **T** 552 4045. *Mon-Fri 0900-1830, Sat 1000-1600, closed Sun*.

Police
The main police station is at Hverfisgata 113-5, **T** 569 9020, opposite the Hlemmur bus station. In the centre there's also a police station at Tryggvagata 19, **T** 569 9025. If you need urgent assistance dial **T** 112.

Post offices
Central Post Office, Pósthússtræti 5, 101 Reykjavík, **T** 580 1101. *Mon-Fri 0900-1630*. Includes poste restante. A letter/postcard to the UK costs ISK 60 for up to 50 g, to the rest of Europe ISK 85, and outside Europe ISK 135. Post boxes are red, marked *Posturinn*.

Public holidays
Banks, businesses and shops are closed on the following days: **New Year's Day**, **Maundy Thursday** (Thu before Easter), **Good Friday**, **Easter Sunday**, **Easter Monday**, **First Day of Summer** (3rd Thu in Apr), **Labour Day** (1 May), **Ascension Day**, **Whitsunday**, **Whitmonday**, **National Day** (17 Jun), **Bank Holiday** (1st Mon in Aug), **Christmas Eve** (from 1200), **Christmas Day**, **Boxing Day**, **New Year's Eve**.

Religious services
Dómkirkjan, catholic church at Austurvöllur, **T** 551 2113. *Mon-Fri 1000-1700*. Masses on Sun at 1100. **Kaþólska kirkjan**, catholic church at Túngata, **T** 552 5388. Masses in English Sun 1800, in Icelandic Mon-Fri 1800, Sun 1030, 1400. **Hallgrímskirkja**, Skólavörðuholt, **T** 510 1000. Masses on Sun 1100 year round.

Student organizations
University of Iceland, Suðurgata, 101 Reykjavík, **T** 525 4593, www.hi.is.

Tax (VAT) refunds
If you buy goods for over ISK 4000 from one shop, you are entitled to a partial tax refund which can be obtained either at the airport or at *The Centre*, see p35. For further information see www.icelandrefund.is.

Taxi firms
Borgarbílastöðin, **T** 552 2440. **BSH Taxis**, **T** 555 0888. **BSR Taxis**, **T** 561 0000, www.bsr.is.**Taxi Hreyfill**, Fellsmúla 26-28, 108 Reykjavík, **T** 588 5523, www.hreyfill.is/english.

Telephone
Austurvöllur telegraph office phone booths open Mon-Fri 0815-1900, Sat-Sun 1000-1800. You can use coins or cards. A local call costs ISK 30 and then ISK 1 per minute thereafter. Overseas calls cost ISK 50, then ISK 30 per minute thereafter. The cheapest overseas calls can be made from the **Atlas Phone Centre** on the 2nd floor of *The Centre*, see p35. **T** 00 for overseas calls, **T** 115 for assistance, **T** 118 for directory enquiries and **T** 114 for information on finding a phone number abroad. All numbers in Iceland have 7 digits. Icelandic phone books are found beside public phones and list residents by their first name and profession.

Tent hire
Útilíf, BSÍ bus station, Vatnsmýrarvegur 10, 101 Reykjavík, **T** 551 7830. A 2-3 person tent costs from ISK 3500 for 2 days, ISK 5500 for 6 days, ISK 350 for each extra day. Book at least 1 day in advance.

Time
Greenwich Mean Time year round.

Tipping
No tipping is required for any form of transport or in any bar or restaurant.

Toilets
Public toilets at the Lækjargata end of Bankastræti and in the City Hall, on the first floor.

Transport enquiries
BSÍ coach terminal, Vatnsmýrarvegur, **T** 552 2300. **Flybus**, **T** 562 1011.

Travel agents
Destination Iceland, Lágmúli 4, 108 Reykjavík, **T** 585 4270, www.dice.is. *15 May-15Aug Mon-Fri 0700-1900, Sat 1000-1400; 16 Aug-14 May Mon-Fri 0900-1700.* For tours, independent travel, flights, bus tickets and various packages. **Hostelling in Iceland**, Icelandic Youth Hostel Association, Sundlaugavegur 34, 105 Reykjavík, **T** 553 8110, www.hostel.is. Information for the 23 hostels across Iceland in addition to a travel service and cheap car rental. **Icelandic Farm Holidays**, Sidumuli 2, 108 Reykjavík, **T** 570 2700, www.farmholidays.is. Accommodation in 120 farms across the country with self-drive packages and rustic charm guaranteed. **Stúdentaferðir**, Bankastræti 10, 101 Reykjavík, **T** 562 2362, www.exit.is. Student travel bureau offering cheaper international flights. See also Student organizations on p217.

A sprint through history

c300 BC	Explorer Pytheas of Massalia reports the discovery of Thule, or Ultima Thule, the northernmost island in the world, six days by sea north of the British Isles and the name subsequently crops up in Greek and Roman sources. It is unknown whether he was definitely referring to Iceland, but Thule is known to be the oldest name for the country, used in the Middle Ages.
c300 AD	Roman coins dating from this time have been found in the south and southeast of Iceland. Nobody knows their exact provenance, although it is thought that they may have arrived with settlers in the ninth and tenth centuries.
795 AD	Irish hermits believed to have been living in Iceland by this time. An Irish monk writes of some Irish priests who lived for a time on a remote uninhabited island called Thule where there was bright sunlight during the day and night. The monks are not thought to have settled on the island permanently, although it is certain that they were around before the Vikings.
c850 AD	Viking explorers chance upon Iceland. Norwegian Viking Flóki Vilgerdarson dubbed it Iceland when he came upon a fjord full of ice in winter. None of the explorers chose to settle and instead reported back to fellow Vikings in Norway about the country.
c874-7 AD	Following a quarrel, Ingólfur Arnarson escapes tyranny of Norwegian King Harald Finehair and

settles in Iceland. He is credited with being the first settler of the country.

870-930 AD The Age of Settlement when the uninhabited areas of the country were claimed and settled. The events of this time are recorded in the *Book of Settlements* and the *Book of Icelanders*. By 930 AD the population was around 60,000.

930 AD The independent Icelandic Commonwealth is established. The Alþing parliament is introduced and held at Þingvellir where the country's 36 municipalities can meet.

930-1030 The Saga Age. A period of national growth when the heroic events celebrated in the sagas unfolded.

c980 AD Greenland discovered by Eiríkur Þorvaldsson, or Erik the Red. He settled there in 986 AD.

1000 The Viking's pagan gods are renounced as Iceland becomes a Christian nation in order to maintain the peace as it is threatened by religious divisions.

c1000 Leifur Eiríksson, or Leif Ericson the Lucky, son of Erik the Red, is believed to have discovered America, which he called Vínland.

1022 Reciprocal agreement made with Norway about sharing wood and water when the Icelanders travelled by ship to Norway.

1030-1118 Period of Peace. Iceland settles down as a Christian nation.

1104 Mount Hekla erupts burying everything within 50 km.

1220-62	Commonweath of Iceland dissolved as Norwegian monarchy grows in power and certain Icelandic clans gathers political and economic power.
1263	King Magnús of Norway establishes codes of law for Iceland.
1383	As the son of King Hákon of Norway and Iceland and Princess Margaret, daughter of the king of Denmark, Oluf inherits all three countries when his father dies. He is six years old. This marks the beginning of the ties between these nations.
1536	The Reformation exerts a huge impact in Denmark causing a revolt against the king. Christian III becomes the king and formally establishes the Lutheran church in Iceland, Denmark and the Faroe Islands.
1627	Algerian pirates attack the Westman Isles, plundering valuables, killing people and taking hundreds of people as slaves to be sold in North Africa.
1662	The King of Denmark, Frederick II, changes the government to become absolute monarch of Iceland, Denmark and Norway.
1749	Skúli Magnússon becomes the first Icelandic bailiff after a succession of Danish bailiffs and establishes workshops and industry in Reykjavík, allowing it to grow beyond a small village. New industries include fishing, agriculture, wool manufacture and mining.

1783-84	The terrible eruptions of Katla (1755) and Hekla (1766) are topped by the Laki eruptions beginning in spring 1783 and lasting a year, said to have created the world's largest lava field in historical times by a single eruption. Toxic gas, starvation and the eruption itself reduces the population to about 40,000. Between 9000 and 10,000 people are said to have died from hunger alone.
1814	The union of Norway and Iceland is dissolved following a Norwegian revolt against the Danish king.
1843	The Alþing is restored as Icelanders successfully petition the Danish king for their own assembly.
1849	The Danish king alters the constitution after popular demonstrations to replace absolute monarchy. Iceland is not directly affected but the movement towards independence has begun.
1870-1914	Between 10,000 and 20,000 Icelanders emigrate to North America, mainly Canada, as Iceland is persistently ravaged by earthquakes and volcanoes which destroy valuable farmland.
1874	The millennium of settlement is celebrated. The Danish king brings a constitution for the country for the celebration allowing legislative and financial power to rest with the Alþing but all laws still have to be signed by the king himself.
1904	Executive power of the government is transferred from Copenhagen to Reykjavík.

1918	Iceland is granted freedom as a sovereign state of Denmark in the Act of Union.
1940	The British occupy Iceland peacefully during the Second World War as a strategic location in the middle of the North Atlantic. Later the Americans replace the British.
1944	Iceland is proclaimed a republic on 17 June after political changes in Denmark as a result of the Second World War.
1945	The Keflavík Treaty is agreed whereby the US is allowed to lease the strategically important military base in Keflavík for a period of 99 years.
1949	Iceland gains membership to NATO.
1952-77	Cod wars waged with Britain, Germany and other nations fishing in the North Atlantic to preserve Icelandic fishing waters. Iceland is victorious.
1955	Halldór Laxness wins the Nobel Prize for Literature with his novel *Independent People* about rural life in Iceland.
1970	Iceland joins the European Free Trade Association (EFTA)
1972	World Chess Champsionship takes place in Iceland between American Bobby Fischer and Russian Boris Spassky, at the height of the Cold War; Fischer wins.
1980	Vigdís Finnbogadóttir becomes the President of Iceland, the first female and single mother to become a president anywhere in the world.

1985	Iceland declares itself a nuclear-free zone.
1972	World Chess Championships take place in Reykjavík between American Bobby Fischer and Russian Boris Spassky. Fischer wins and it is hailed a Cold War victory.
1992	Iceland leaves the International Whaling Committee (IWC) in protest at what it sees as the IWC's anti-whaling stance.
2000	Reykjavík is proclaimed one of the European cities of culture.
2002	By a narrow margin of 19 votes to 18, Iceland is readmitted to the IWC.
2003	Iceland engages in its first whale hunt for 15 years claiming it is for scientific reasons and aims to study the mammals' impact on fish stocks.
2004	The Grimsvotn volcano erupts, scattering ash as far away as Finland. The volcano is in a remote part of the island and there are no casualties.
2006	Iceland is scheduled to restart commercial whaling.
2007	The next national parliamentary elections will take place in May.

Books

Iceland is built on a foundation of literature which has consist-ently recorded the feuds, parliaments and farming disputes since settlers first reached Iceland's shores and the sagas hold a dear place in the country's cultural history. Halldór Laxness dominates the contemporary literary scene, whose work is characterized by an extra dry, sarcastic humour and a lot of weirdness. There are a number of novels that have recently been translated into English. Icelandic books are very expensive even though the country publishes more books per capita than any other nation. Some are also still hard to get hold of outside the country but should be able to be imported through major bookshops.

Biographies

McDonnell, Evelyn, *Army of She: Icelandic, Iconoclastic, Irrepressible Björk* (2001), Random House. Spiky, punky and quick-fire autobiography of Iceland's most famous face.

Contemporary fiction

Guðmundsson, Einar Már, *Angels of the Universe* (1997) St Martin's Press. Translation. Ethereal modern Icelandic of spirituality and nature recently made into a film that will take your breath away.

Helgason, H, *101 Reykjavík* (2002), Faber & Faber. Hilarious hip tale of lesbianism, suicide, the futility of life, and the bars and clubs of the city. Recently turned into an award-winning film.

Kárason, E, *Devil's Island* (2000), Canongate Books. Rural sentiments and ways of life clash harshly with the Americans who descend on the Keflavík Airbase in Iceland.

Laxness, H, *Independent People* (1946, reprinted 2001), Harvill Press. Halldór Laxness won the Nobel Prize for Literature in 1955 for this outstanding novel about a farmer's struggle against the elements and other forces in the unforgiving countryside of Iceland. Highly recommended. By the same author are: *Paradise Reclaimed* (1960, reprinted 2002), Vintage Books USA; *The Atom Station* (1948, reprinted 2004), Harvill Press; and *The Fish Can Sing* (1957, reprinted 2001), Harvill Press, in which a young Icelandic boy is caught up in the celebrity of an Icelandic musician who makes it big abroad and becomes a local hero.

Ólafsson, Ó, *The Journey Home*, (2001), Anchor Books. An Icelandic woman working in England in the late fifties decides to leave the country to seek her land of birth. A moving tale of homecoming.

Verne, J, *Journey to the Centre of the Earth*, (1864, reprinted 1991), Bantam Books. A scientist discovers a cryptic manuscript which leads him to a whole new world hidden beneath a dormant volcano in Iceland.

Travelogues

Armitage, S, and **Maxwell**, G, *Moon Country* (1996), Faber & Faber. Head and shoulders above the few travelogues available on the country, poets Armitage and Maxwell trace the steps of WH Auden around the country and find much to write about.

Auden, W H, and **MacNeice**, L, *Letters from Iceland* (1937), Faber & Faber. A collection of poems, letters and narrative about a journey made by the two poets as young men.

Millman, L, *Last Places – A Journey in the North* (1990), Houghton Mifflin. Millman follows the Viking route from Scotland to Newfoundland via Iceland and Greenland. Entertaining and readable.

Moore, T, *Frost on My Moustache* (2000), Abacus. Lad-mag writer Moore treks around Iceland following the path of the Marquess of Dufferin, a Victorian sailor who sailed to Iceland and the Arctic Circle in 1856. Occasionally amusing.

Photographic books

Roberts, D, and **Krakauer**, J, *Iceland: Land of the Sagas* (1990), Villard. Inspirational photography and informative writing about Iceland's history, landscape and sagas.

Sigurjónsson, S, *Lost in Iceland* (2002), Forlagið Publishing. Beautiful book of photography showing Iceland's varied and rich environment. The best a number of coffee table books available.

Travel guides

Sullivan, P, *Waking up in Iceland* (2003), Sanctuary. A guide to Iceland's happening music scene. Also provides information on Reykjavík's sights and culture, in a cool and contemporary way.

History

Byock, J L, *Viking Age Iceland*, (2001), Penguin. History, archaeology and anthropology blended to re-evaluate Viking behaviour and challenge long-held notions that they were merely violent and unsophisticated.

Hjálmarsson, J R, *History of Iceland: from the Settlement to the Present Day*, (1993), Iceland Review. Bite-size, readable history of the country.

Karlsson, G, *Iceland's 1100 Years: History of a marginal society*, (2000), Mál og Menning. Detailed account of the growth of the nation, particularly its oppression and poverty.

Geography

Guðmundsson, A T, and **Kjartansson**, H, *Guide to the Geology of Iceland* (1984), Örn og Örlygur. A comprehensive guide to Iceland's geology with an explanation of features such as volcanoes, glaciers, plate tectonics and geothermal activity. By the same authors, *Earth in Action* (1996) Vaka-Helgafell,

Architecture

Guide to Icelandic architecture (2000), Association of Icelandic Architects. Looks at the history and development of architecture in Iceland, including over 250 buildings.

The Icelandic Sagas

More than a collection of old stories glorifying the Viking past, the Icelandic sagas are a work of medieval art, the cornerstone of the country's culture and a piece of living history. While shamelessly hamming up aspects of the raiding, trading and gold-hoarding Nordic travellers, these calfskin manuscripts have lovingly preserved familial bonds through their genealogies and have given a relatively recent culture a full documentation of their history from the first settler onwards. Although not 100

! JRR Tolkien had a number of Icelandic nannies to look after his children in England because he was interested in their retelling of the old saga tales. *Oðin's Saga*, for example, contains references to powerful rings that can multiply and be used to rule the world.

percent reliable in terms of historical fact – they are a dramatisation of events after all – the sagas have played a major role in establishing genetic links among the family-tree hunting Icelanders and the director of a Reykjavík genetics institute has even traced his own ancestry back to Égill Skallagrímsson. Historians have used the vivid period detail to recreate the Viking's vengeful world and there is no finer way to involve yourself in the ancient world than to step back a thousand years with one of the excellent translations. Reykjavík's excellent Saga Museum and Árni Magnússon Institute can also take your interest further.

Various, *Sagas of Icelanders* (2000), Penguin. This is the full authoritative collection of the Icelandic sagas translated into English. Listed below are three of the most gripping sagas available singly – stories of Viking raids, attacks, revenge and buried treasure.

Cook, R, *Njal's Saga* (2001), Penguin Classics. Translation. Written by an unknown 13th century author, Njal's Saga is one of the classics of the genre. The tale centres on a fifty year feud and the prophetic figure of Njal Þorgeirsson who comes to a bitter end. Family honour, integrity and the revenge culture are fully explored in this depiction of a society who created their own social laws with a punishment of death for all infringements.

Edwards, P, and **Pálsson**, H, *Égill's Saga* (1976), Penguin Classics. Translation. If you only ever read one saga, read the Saga of Égill. His story begins with his life as an unruly and murderous child, seemingly born into the body of an older boy, who rapidly becomes a well-respected Viking warrior. Égill uses his gift of poetry to get him off the hook when he is sentenced to death.

Even at his eventual death he has the last laugh, riding off into the distance to bury his gold. He's a complex character and the story is somewhere between a Viking romp and an epic work of poetry.

Faulkes, Anthony and **Johnston**, George *Three Icelandic Outlaw Sagas: The Saga of Gisli, The Saga of Grettir, The Saga of Hord* (2001), Phoenix Press. Translation. Three stories of epic adventure with the common theme of the outlaw at their heart. Grettir is a typically impetuous and very likeable character, Hord is an orphan and Gisli wields a sword called Greyflank. If you've ever wondered where the Icelandic love of the underdog originated, examine these outsiders closely and you'll find out.

Magnusson, M, and **Pálsson**, H, *Laxdæla Saga* (1976), Penguin Classics. Translation. While many narrative threads intertwine in the Laxdæla Saga, the most striking is that of the beautiful daughter of Gudrun Osvif who is forced to marry the best friend of her true love. The scenario and its tragic denouement owe much to European chivalric literature of the early medieval period, but the violence and strength at the heart of the female character is typically Icelandic. In this society, women are at least equal to men.

Magnusson, M, and **Pálsson**, H, *The Vinland Sagas: The Norse Discovery of America, Grænlendinga Saga, Eirik's Saga* (1965), Penguin Classics. Translation. Five hundred years before Christopher Columbus, Leif the Lucky discovered Vinland, thought to have been Newfoundland. Like his father Erik the Red before him, Leif was an inspirational explorer and the Vinland Sagas tell the stories of Leif, Erik and their discovery and travel through the unexplored territories of Greenland and the North American Continent.

Language

Icelandic is spoken by less than 300,000 people worldwide and Icelanders are rightly proud of their language. But it's a tricky language to master and because so few foreigners speak it the locals find it hard to understand the words spoken in a foreign accent, so it's often much easier to speak English. TV, films and music all mean that English is spoken near perfectly here, but there's little danger of the Icelandic language dying out itself.

Committees are put together to prevent the language from absorbing non-native words so when new technologies reach the country new compound words are created from older saga words for them. Telephone, for example, is *simi*, meaning a thread; TV is *sjónvarp*, meaning thrown picture and computer is *tölva*, meaning prophetess of numbers. A few basic words and phrases are given below, with a pronounciation guide in parenthesis.

If you want to learn the language your options are limited. Even when you have mastered the complex grammatical system – a bit like German and also Swedish – you'll find that most Icelanders speak English and that the language is only used by little over 300,000 people in the world today. Still, there is an undeniable poetry in the closest surviving relative to the Viking language, Old Norse, and the small selection of primers are thankfully not too unwieldy or over-complicated.

Glendening, PJT, *Teach Yourself Icelandic* (1993), Hodder and Stoughton. Useful lesson-based book for beginner students of the written language.

Neijmann, Daisy L, *Colloquial Icelandic: The Complete Course for Beginners* (Colloquial Series). Comprehensive tape, CD and textbook-based course based on spoken everyday Icelandic. Lessons and exercises lead you through the basics as a beginner towards a thorough understanding of the language.

Berlitz Scandinavian Cassette Pack (1996). 75 minute cassette and phrase book covering the (very) basics of Icelandic in addition to Danish, Finnish, Norwegian and Swedish. Learn to say "Stop thief!" and "I'd like a hot chocolate" in five Scandinavian languages.

A quick guide to pronunciation.

Icelandic is not an easy language to pronounce and nothing sounds quite as it looks on the page. This is a brief guide to the key differences between English and Icelandic ways of pronouncing letters.

A ah
Á ow
Ð/ð eth, pronounced like th in the
I ea
Í ee
L chlh, similar to the Welsh pronunciation of ll
R always rolled
Þ thorn, pronounced like th in think
Æ ai
Ö oeah

Basic words and phrases

Good morning *Góðan dag/Gott daginn*   (Go-athan dach/gott dayinn)
Goodbye *Bless*   (Bless)
Yes *Já*   (Yow)
No *Nei*   (Neigh)
Thanks *Takk fyrir/ Takk*   (Takk firir)
Excuse me/sorry *Afsakið*   (Af-sah-kith)
Do you speak english? *Talarðu ensku?*   (Tal-ar-oo ensku)
I don't know *Ég skil ekki*   (Yeg skil ekki)

Where is..? *Hvar er…?* (Kvar er)
Can you help me? *Geturðu hjálpað mér?* (Get-urthu heyalpath mier)
What's the time? *Hvað er klukkan?* (Kvath er klukkan)
How much does… cost? *Hvað kostar..?* (Kvath kostar)
Where is the bathroom? *Hvar er klósettið?* (Kvar er klausettith)
When does…open? *Hvernær opnar…?* (Kvertner opnar)
When does… close? *Hvernær lokar…?* (Kvertner lokkar)
I would like… *Ég ætla að fá…* (Yeg etla ath fow)

Emergencies

Help! *Hjálp!* (Heyowlp!)
I feel ill *Mér líður illa* (Mier lee-thur itla)
I need a doctor *Ég þarf lækni* (Yeg tharf like-ni)

Eating out

I don't eat meat *Ég borða ekki kjöt* (Yeg bortha ekki kjoht)
What do you want to drink? *Hvað viltu drekka?* (Kvath viltoo drekka)
A beer please *Bjórglas, takk* (Be-or glass takk)
Cheers! *Skál!* (Scowl!)

Icelandic specialities
Svið Singed sheep's head
Sviðasulta Sheep's head jelly/paté
Hangikjöt Smoked lamb
Blóðmör Black pudding
Lifrapylsa Liver pudding
Ýmis súrmatur Various soured meats
Selshreifar Seal's flipper
Hrútspungar Ram's testicles
Saltkjöt Salted lamb

Flatkökur, flatbrauð Rye pancakes, flatbread
Hákarl Rotten shark
Harðfiskur Dried fish, often cod
Skyr Thick yoghurt
Ávaxtaskyr Skyr with fruit

Kjöt Meat

Lamb Lamb
Naut Beef
Svín Pork
Folald Foal
Hreindýr Reindeer
Hamborgarhryggur Smoked saddle of pork
London lamb Lightly smoked lamb
Kjötfars Sausage meat, meatballs
Hryggvöðvi (filé) Fillet
Súpakjöt Meat stew
Skinka Ham
Beikon Bacon
Saltkjöt Salted meat
Reykt kjöt Smoked meat
Kálfasneið Veal schnitzel
Hangikjöt Smoked lamb
Pylsur Sausages

Fuglar Birds

Rjúpa Ptarmigan
Lundi Puffin
Reyktur Lundi Smoked Puffin
Svartfugl Guillemot
Kjúklingur Chicken
Hænuegg Hen's egg
Svartfuglsegg Seabird's egg
Andaregg Duck's egg

Fiskur Fish
Ýsa Haddock
Þorskur Cod
Lúða Halibut
Sandhverfa Turbot
Skarholi Plaice
Karfi Redfish
Skata Skate
Skötuselur Monkfish
Steinbítur Catfish
Langa Ling
Rauðmagi Lumpfish
Síld Herring
Saltfiskur Salt cod or haddock
Lax Salmon
Silungur Trout
Bleikja Arctic char
Áll Eel
Hörpuskel Scallop
Kræklingur Mussel
Humar Lobster
Rækja Shrimp

Fruit and vegetables
Eppli Apple
Appelsina Orange
Jarðarber Strawberry
Tómatur Tomato
Vinber Grapes
Baunir Beans or peas
Laukur Onion
Kartöflur Potatoes

Drinks
Té Tea
Kaffee Coffee
Mjólk Milk
Bjór Beer
Hvít vín White wine
Rauð vín Red wine
Gos Fizzy drink (or volcanic eruption)
Vatn Water

Other
Kaka Cake
Brauð Bread
Samloka Sandwich
Sykkur Sugar
Ís Ice cream
Súpa Soup

Index

Credits

Publishing stuff

Footprint credits
Editor and researcher: Nicola Jones
Map editor: Sarah Sorensen
Picture editor: Rob Lunn

Publisher: Patrick Dawson
Series created by: Rachel Fielding
In-house cartography: Claire Benison,
Kevin Feeney,
Design: Mytton Williams

Maps: adapted from original cartography
by PCGraphics (UK) Ltd

Photography credits
Front cover: Alamy
Inside: Nordic Photos, Laura Dixon
Generic images: John Matchett
Back cover: Nordic Photos

Print
Manufactured in Italy by LegoPrint
Pulp from sustainable forests

Footprint feedback
We try as hard as we can to make
each Footprint guide as up to date as
possible but, of course, things always
change. If you want to let us know
about your experiences – good, bad
or ugly – then don't delay, go to
www.footprintbooks.com and send
in your comments.

® Footprint Handbooks and the Footprint
mark are a registered trademark of
Footprint Handbooks Ltd

Publishing information
Footprint Reykjavík
2nd edition
Text and maps
© Footprint Handbooks Ltd
February 2006

ISBN 1 904777 66 X
CIP DATA: a catalogue record for this
book is available from the British Library

Published by Footprint Handbooks
6 Riverside Court
Lower Bristol Road
Bath, BA2 3DZ, UK
T +44 (0)1225 469141
F +44 (0)1225 469461
discover@footprintbooks.com
www.footprintbooks.com

Distributed in the USA by Publishers
Group West

All rights reserved. No part of this
publication may be reproduced, stored
in a retrieval system, or transmitted, in
any form or by any means, electronic,
mechanical, photocopying recording, or
otherwise without the prior permission
of Footprint Handbooks Ltd.

Every effort has been made to ensure
that the facts in this pocket Handbook
are accurate. However, the authors and
publishers cannot accept responsibility
for any loss, injury or inconvenience
sustained by any traveller as a result
of information or advice contained in
this guide.

242

Acknowledgements

On updating this guide Nicola Jones would particularly like to thank Dóra Magnúsdóttir from Reykjavík Complete and Ian Bradley from Icelandair for their help and information, both before and during the trip. Special thanks also to Nanni Gunnarsdóttir at This is Iceland for all her time, and to Mladen Stific for his insightful views on guidebooks and for making the trip memorable. A big thank you to Laura Dixon and to all at Footprint for the fantastic opportunity to visit Iceland. Finally, many thanks to dad for the extra jumpers and, of course, to the lovely Robin.

Laura Dixon would like to thank the many people who helped with the research of this book. This second edition would not have been possible without the hard work and expert research of Nicola Jones, who also edited the guide, and I'm really glad that she had the chance to see what still is my favourite country in the world. Thanks to the Icelandic tourist offices in Reykjavík, Akureyri and Vestmannaeyjar for their excellent advice and assistance and specifically to Sigrún Hlín Sigurðardóttir, Svanhildur Konráðsdóttir and the guys at the Central Reykjavík Tourist Information. Also thanks to Heimir Máu Petersson, Égill Tomásson and Þórunn Larusdóttir for helping me get to grips with culture in Reykjavík. In the UK, thanks to Ian Bradley and Icelandair and Iain Moody at Athole Still International. Thanks to the many friends I made out in Reykjavík, especially Danial Bishop, Larry Schwarz, Deena Zeltser, Jo Bending and Malene Lorentzen, and to Steinunn Björk Piper for being an excellent teacher. Many thanks to Neil Taylor for his passion and dedication to Björk, and his text about her. A special thank you to all at Footprint for their perspiration, inspiration, dedication and direction.

Publishing stuff

Complete title list

Tallinn (P)
Turin (P)
Turkey
Valencia (P)
Verona (P)
Wales

Latin America & Caribbean

Antigua & Leeward
  Islands (P)
Argentina
Barbados (P)
Bolivia
Brazil
Caribbean Islands
Central America & Mexico
Chile
Colombia
Costa Rica
Cuba
Cusco & the Inca Trail
Dominican Republic (P)
Ecuador & Galápagos
Havana (P)
Mexico
Nicaragua
Peru
Rio de Janeiro (P)
South American Handbook
St Lucia (P)
Venezuela

Middle East

Dubai (P)
Jordan
Syria & Lebanon

North America

New York (P)
Vancouver (P)
Western Canada

Discover guides

Belize, Guatemala & Southern Mexico
East Coast Australia
Patagonia
Peru, Bolivia & Ecuador
Vietnam, Cambodia & Laos
Western Canada

Lifestyle guides

European City Breaks
Surfing Britain
Surfing Europe

(P) denotes pocket guide

Publishing stuff

For a different view…
choose a Footprint

Over 100 Footprint travel guides
Covering more than 150 of the world's most exciting
countries and cities in Latin America, the Caribbean, Africa, Indian
sub-continent, Australasia, North America, Southeast Asia, the
Middle East and Europe.

Discover so much more…
The finest writers. In-depth knowledge. Entertaining and
accessible. Critical restaurant and hotels reviews. Lively
descriptions of all the attractions. Get away from the crowds.

Map 1 Reykjavík

To Viðey

SUNDAHÖFN

Laugardalur Swimming Pool & Spa

0 metres 500
0 yards 500

N

Ásmundur Sveinsson Sculpture Museum

To Grótta Beach

Reykjavík Harbour

Sólfar Sculpture

Höfði

Sæbraut
Borgartún

Laugavegur

Kringlan Mall

Myrargata
Geirsgata
Vesturgata

Lækjartorg Square

Hverfisgata
Laugavegur

Hallgrímskirkja

Kjarvalsstaðir

Miklabraut

Hringbraut

National & University Library

Tjörnin

National Museum of Iceland

Hringbraut

BSÍ Bus Terminal

Perlan

Árni Magnússon Institute

Nordic House

ÖSKJUHLÍÐ HILL

Reykjavík City Airport

Skerjafjörður

Fossvogur

Nauthólsvík Beach

248

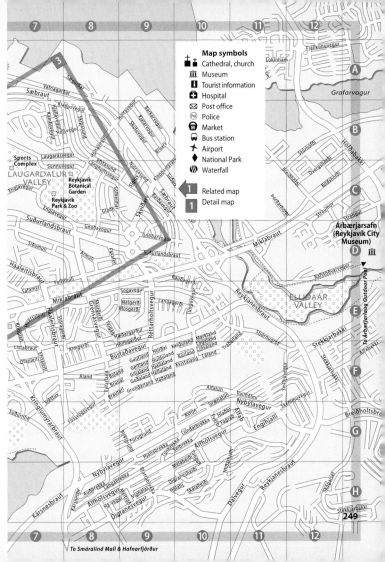

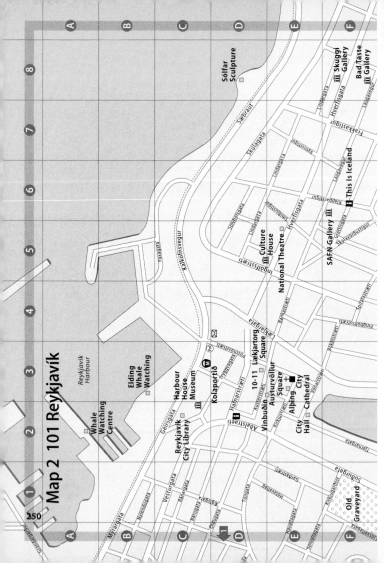

Map 2 101 Reykjavik

250

Reykjavík Harbour

Sólfar Sculpture

Skuggi Gallery

Bad Taste Gallery

This Is Iceland

SAFN Gallery

Culture House

National Theatre

Whale Watching Centre

Elding Whale Watching

Harbour House Museum

Kolaportið

Reykjavik City Library

Vínbúðin

10–11

Lækjartorg Square

Austurvöllur Square

Alþing

City Cathedral

City Hall

Old Graveyard

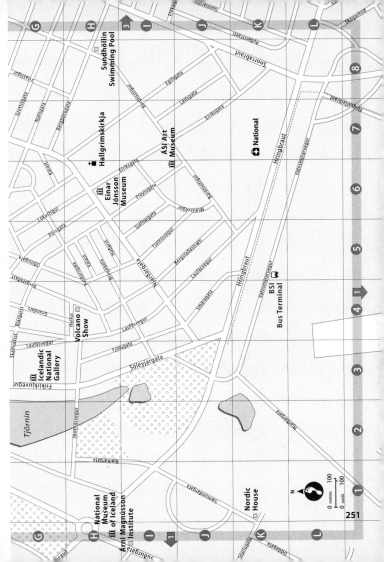

Sundhöllin
Swimming Pool

Hallgrímskirkja

Einar
Jónsson
Museum

ÁSÍ Art
Museum

National

Volcano
Show

Icelandic
National
Gallery

BSÍ
Bus Terminal

Tjörnin

National
Museum
of Iceland

Árni Magnússon
Institute

Nordic
House

Sóleyjargata

Fríkirkjuvegur

Laufásvegur

Njarðargata

Hringbraut

Vatnsmýrarvegur

Snorrabraut

Bergstaðastræti

Freyjugata

Mímisvegur

Eiríksgata

Eiríksgata

Egilsgata

Leifsgata

Njarðargata

Baldursgata

Lokastígur

Þórsgata

Óðinsgata

Bragagata

Týsgata

Urðarstígur

Spítalastígur

Fjólugata

Skothúsvegur

Bjarkargata

Sóleyjargata

Sóleyjargata

Skálholtsstígur

Bergstaðastræti

Grundarstígur

Hellir

Vitastígur

Frakkastígur

Bergþórugata

Grettisgata

Njálsgata

Skólavörðustígur

Smáragata

Fjólugata

Laufásvegur

Garðastræti

Öskjuhlíð

Skeggjagata

Auðarstræti

Flókagata

Gunnarsbraut

Sæmundargata

Oddagata

Suðurgata

Sturlugata

Skerjafjörður

N

0 metres 100
0 yards 100

251

G H I J K L

1 2 3 4 5 6 7 8

Map 3 Laugardalur Valley

A
B
C
D
E
F
G
H

1 2 3 4 5 6

Laugalækur
Laugarnesvegur
Hrísateigur
Kirkjuteigur
Hofteigur
Laugateigur
Sigtún

Sæbraut
Höfði
Borgartún

Skúlagata
Sætún
Samtún
Miðtún
Söltún
Miðtún
Hátún
Hátún

Kringlumýrarbraut

Skúlagata
Höfðatún
Mýrargata
Grettisgata
Njálsgata
Brautarholt

Mýrin

Bergthorugata
Snorrabraut
Skeggjagata
Gunnarsbraut
Háteigsvegur
Flókagata

Egilsgata
Leifsgata

Laugavegur
Laugavegur
Skipholt
Nóatún
Stangarholt
Einholt
Meðalholt

Háaleitisbraut
Háteigsvegur

Engjateigur

III
Kjarvalsstaðir
Úthlíð
Stakkahlíð
Bolstaðarhlíð
Skaftahlíð
Langahlíð

Kringlumýrarbraut
Lágmúli
Álftamýri
Starmýri
Safamýri

Miklabraut
Barmahlíð
Mávahlíð
Drápuhlíð
Blönduhlíð
Hamrahlíð
Grænahlíð
Stakkahlíð
Reykjahlíð
Eskihlíð
Stigahlíð
Bústaðavegur
Fugallarvegur

**Kringlan
Mall**

Stigahlíð
Kringlumýrarbraut
Kringlan
Heigjasalir

252 **Perlan**
Háahlíð

ÖSKJUHLÍÐ
HILL

1 2 3 4 5 6

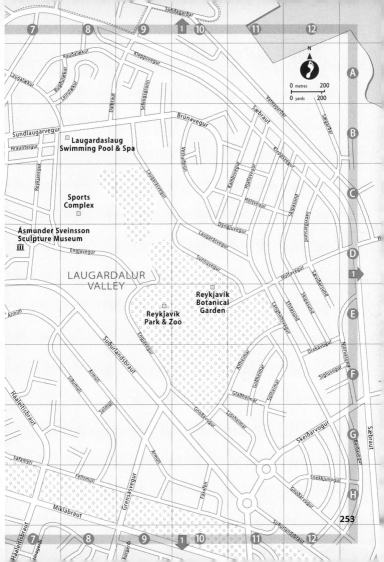

Ⓐ
Ⓑ
Ⓒ
Ⓓ
➤①
Ⓔ
Ⓕ
Ⓖ
Ⓗ

N

0 metres 200
0 yards 200

Sundagarðar
Raudalækur
Kleppsvegur
Laugalækur
Laugarnesvegur
Rauðalækur
Dalbraut
Kirkjuteigur
Brúnavegur
Sæbraut
Yrlatangur
Dugguvogur
Sundlaugavegur
Hraunteigur
Reykjavegur
Kleppsvegur

**Laugardaslaug
Swimming Pool & Spa**

Laugarásvegur
Kambsvegur
Hrísateigur
Hrísateigur
Hofsvegur
Þinghólt

**Sports
Complex**

Dynjuvegur
Laugarásvegur
Vesturhlíð

**Ásmundar Sveinsson
Sculpture Museum**

Engjavegur
Laugarásvegur
Sunnuvegur
Hofsvegur
Skipasund
Sæviðarsund

**LAUGARDALUR
VALLEY**

**Reykjavík
Botanical
Garden**

**Reykjavík
Park & Zoo**

Dagmettavegur
Sæviðarsund
Skipasund
Engjavegur
Ármúli
Suðurlandsbraut
Ármúli
Drekavogur
Álfheimar
Sigluvogur
Nóatún
Sæviðarsund

Glaðheimar
Sólheimar
Goðheimar
Ljósheimar
Skeiðarvogur
Sæbraut
Barðavogur
Ármúli
Selmúli
Síðumúli
Suðurlandsbraut
Ármúli
Fáafen
Snekkjuvogur
Gnoðarvogur

Háaleitisbraut
Safamýri
Grensásvegur
Fellsmúli
Miklabraut
Vogakjör
Suðurlandsbraut

253

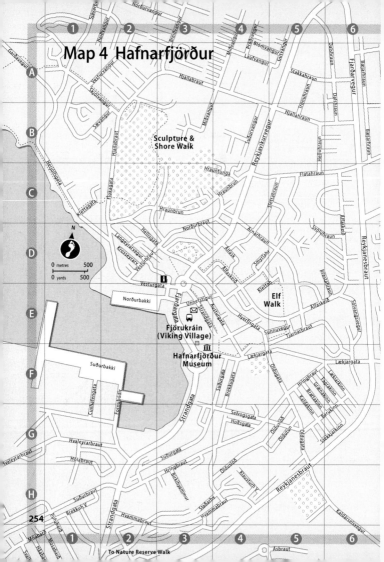

Map 4 Hafnarfjörður

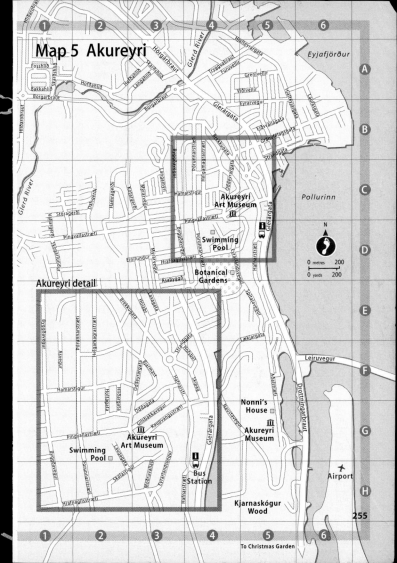

Map 5 Akureyri

Eyjafjörður

Glerá River

Pollurinn

Akureyri
Art Museum

Swimming
Pool

Botanical
Gardens

N

0 metres 200
0 yards 200

Akureyri detail

Akureyri
Art Museum

Swimming
Pool

Bus
Station

Nonni's
House

Akureyri
Museum

Leiruvegur

Airport

Kjarnaskógur
Wood

To Christmas Garden

255

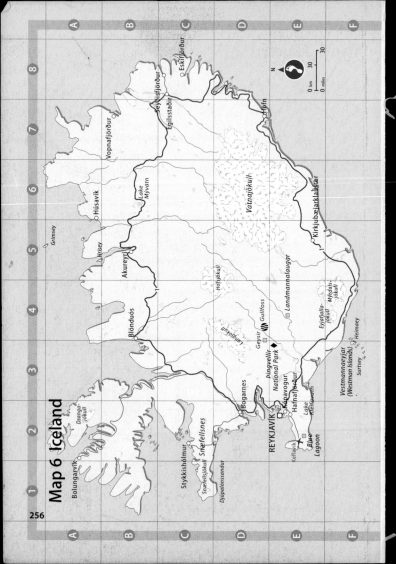

Map 6 Iceland

256

Summer
Exhibition
List of Works
2013

Royal
Academy
of Arts